Puerto Rico

Puerto Rico

Lucile Davis

Children's Press®
A Division of Scholastic Inc.
New York   Toronto   London   Auckland   Sydney
Mexico City   New Delhi   Hong Kong
Danbury, Connecticut

Frontispiece: Puerto Rican National Forest Quebrada Juan

Front cover: Old San Juan, Castillo de San Felipe del Morro

Back cover: Puerto Rican beach

Consultant: Lydia Santana, M.L.S., Luquillo High School

Please note: All statistics are as up-to-date as possible at the time of publication.

Book production by Editorial Directions, Inc.

Library of Congress Cataloging-in-Publication Data

Davis, Lucile.
  Puerto Rico / Lucile Davis.
     144 p. 24 cm.
  Includes bibliographical references and index.
  Summary : Describes the geography, plants, animals, history, economy, religions, culture, sports, arts, and people of Puerto Rico.
  ISBN 0-516-21042-4
  1. Puerto Rico—Juvenile literature. [1. Puerto Rico.] I. Title.
F1958.3.D38 2000
972.95—dc21   99-26988
                                                                        CIP
                                                                         AC

Acknowledgments

I want to thank the Honorable Carlos Romero Barceló and his congressional staff and the Honorable Kay Granger and her Fort Worth office staff for their valuable assistance with this project. Thanks also to Magaly Rivera and her "Welcome to Puerto Rico" website and the "virtual watercooler crowd" of writers for their help, suggestions, and support. And as always, thanks Mom and Papa.

Waterfalls at El Yunque

Puerto Rican beach

Impatiens in El Yunque

Contents

Coquí

Old San Juan

Central mountains region

Puerto Ricans

Young baseball player

CHAPTER ONE

A Question of Status

With its sun-drenched beaches and sparkling waters, Puerto Rico is, as the Spanish once called it, *La Isla del Encanto*—the Island of Enchantment. Once the Spanish became residents they renamed it Puerto Rico—rich port

Puerto Rico is a commonwealth of the United States. In general, a commonwealth is a group of nations, states, or other political units banded together for the common good. In the case of Puerto Rico, the United States has given the term a somewhat different meaning. Puerto Rico is a self-governing political unit that is, by consent, politically and economically linked to the United States. It receives assistance and protection from the United States government, but the Puerto Rican government has authority over most matters concerning the island.

Citizens of Puerto Rico are also citizens of the United States. Although they do not pay taxes or vote in U.S. presidential elections, they may choose or be required to serve in the U.S. armed

Tourists are drawn to Puerto Rico's sunny beaches.

Opposite: Cerromar Beach

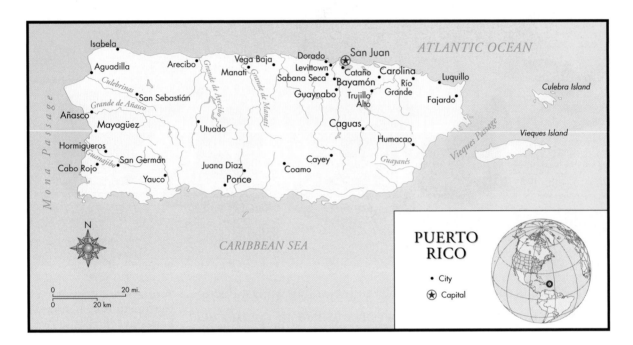

Isabela
Aguadilla
Arecibo
Vega Baja
Dorado
San Juan
ATLANTIC OCEAN
Manatí
Levittown
Cataño
Carolina
Sabana Seca
Bayamón
Río Grande
Luquillo
Culebrinas
San Sebastián
Guaynabo
Trujillo Alto
Fajardo
Culebra Island
Grande de Añasco
Añasco
Mayagüez
Utuado
Caguas
Vieques Passage
Vieques Island
Hormigueros
Humacao
Guanajibo
San Germán
Cayey
Guayanés
Cabo Rojo
Juana Diaz
Coamo
Yauco
Ponce

Mona Passage
Grande de Arecibo
Grande de Manatí

N

CARIBBEAN SEA

0   20 mi.
0   20 km

PUERTO RICO

• City

⊛ Capital

Geopolitical map of Puerto Rico

forces. Visitors from the mainland of the United States don't need a passport to visit the island.

The people of Puerto Rico have much in common with their Caribbean neighbors, who share Spain's culture. Sixteenth-century Spanish explorers searching for wealth created the first European settlements on the islands. The dominant language of the Caribbean, therefore, is Spanish. Although most Puerto Ricans speak Spanish, both Spanish and English are official languages of the island.

When Spain ceded, or granted, Puerto Rico to the United States in 1898, the island began to adopt some of the culture and economics of America. Today, in its major cities, skyscrapers, fast-food outlets, and U.S.-style retail stores tower over open-air markets and squares built by the Spanish centuries ago. In a number of places, modern hotels overlook ancient Spanish forts. Baseball, rock music, and New York fashions can all be found in this United States commonwealth. However, though it may look like life in one of the states, the island is not American—it is Puerto Rican.

The Open Question

Puerto Rico has never been an independent nation, yet it has its own flag, its own anthem, and even its own Olympic team. Though it is economically and politically tied to the United States, the island is considered a model for Latin America.

Many Puerto Ricans enjoy the trade and industry brought by their ties with the United States, but they do not want to be turned into Americans. Others like the close association with the United States and want to make it permanent by becoming a U.S. state.

This debate over status, which began before the turn of the twentieth century, is at the heart of Puerto Rican politics. The first of the modern Puerto Rican political parties, the Popular Democratic Party (PPD), was organized in 1938 to champion the cause of independence. Later, the party's leader, Luis Muñoz Marín, abandoned the fight for independence in favor of a permanent union with the United States. Muñoz Marín believed Puerto Rico's economic development depended on its ties with the United States.

In 1946, the Puerto Rican Independence Party was founded to take up the cause the first party had abandoned—independence. Twenty years later, in August 1967, the New Progressive Party was

Spelling *Puerto*

When U.S. armed forces landed in Puerto Rico in 1898, the general in charge decided that the island's name should be *Porto Rico*, even though there is no such word as *porto* in Spanish. It wasn't until 1932 that the U.S. Congress decided that it really should be *Puerto*—which, of course, the Puerto Ricans had known all along. ■

Puerto Ricans have voted on their status with the United States a number of times.

organized to push for union with the United States as the fifty-first state. On November 14, 1993, the question of status was put to a vote. The election results favored continuing the commonwealth, but by such a small margin that the vote settled nothing.

On December 13, 1998, Puerto Ricans went back to the ballot box to vote again on the question of status. The decision the voters were asked to decide was difficult. Each of the options on the bal-

A Note about Spanish Names

The last names of individuals usually have two parts—the father's name followed by the mother's name, but they are alphabetized under the father's name. For example, three generations of a Puerto Rican family are: Luis Muñoz Rivera; son Luis Muñoz Marín, and granddaughter, Victoria Muñoz Mendoza. ■

lot involved major sacrifices for the people of Puerto Rico. Choosing to become a state could mean becoming more Americanized and losing their own culture. Independence would mean the loss of the security and economic backing of the United States that had made the island a leader in the Caribbean and Latin America. If commonwealth status was the choice, the debate would continue.

How did Puerto Rico become entangled in this question of status? The answer lies in the history of the island, its people, and the political events that brought Puerto Rico to the December 1998 vote.

Casting a ballot in the December 1998 status vote

CHAPTER TWO

Early Discoverers

The history of the island of Puerto Rico begins after the last Ice Age. It was the last place in the Caribbean to be settled by early Native American people. Little is known of these first people, but historians believe they came on crude boats from the North American mainland about 4,000 to 2,000 years ago. These people and their culture were too primitive to leave any clear signs of their existence. Because information about them is so limited, they have been labeled *los Arcaicos*, or the Archaics.

An illustration of Puerto Rico in 1599

The next early discoverers were more advanced and left some evidence of their existence. The name given to them, Arawak, is also applied to a group of tribal people who lived in the northern part of South America. These people, with similar languages and cultures, established settlements from the mouth of the Orinoco River in northeast Venezuela along the coast of the continent, then to a string of small islands known today as the Lesser Antilles. This string of small islands led the Arawak to discover a larger island. They called the beautiful island they discovered Borinquén, "the land of the brave lord."

Stone Age Discoverers

The first group of Arawak to reach what is now Puerto Rico were hunters and gatherers who made high-quality pottery. Though they

Opposite: Christopher Columbus and his crew

were not farmers, they settled in communities and built waterproof houses for protection from the rains and high winds that regularly pelted the island.

Around A.D. 500, another group of Arawak explored and settled the interior of the island. They were skilled craftsworkers who used well-made tools and produced beautiful stonework. They used polished stones to create religious objects and built large plazas for games and religious ceremonies.

Finally, around A.D. 1000, a third group of Arawak arrived. Called the Taíno, they were even more advanced culturally and artistically. They had a well-developed society and made intricate carvings in stone, wood, and clay. Although they were highly skilled in shellwork and gold work, the Taíno were a Stone Age people who did not craft metal or carve stone for weapons. Their weapons were unsharpened stone axes and arrows tipped with sharpened bone or shell.

The Taíno were farmers. They were also good sailors, who traded with other Arawak settlements throughout the islands. They had an organized social structure, were deeply religious, and enjoyed a peaceful existence. They lived in large villages governed by chiefs called *caciques*. Village caciques were under the leadership of a higher island cacique, who ruled during times of war.

A Taíno village was built around a central plaza where the cacique's house stood. The plaza was used for village meetings, celebrations, and military drills. Other open areas were used for a game similar to soccer. The game, which may have had a religious significance, was played between teams of women as well as between teams of men.

Women were important to village life. The Taíno were a matriarchal society—all village caciques inherited their position through the female line. When a cacique died, his sister's son rather than his own son succeeded him. Women had many of the rights that men had, including the right to own property.

The Taíno were peace-loving people. The only threat to their way of life were the Carib people who came from the mainland of South America and attacked Arawak island settlements. The Carib were ferocious fighters and may have been cannibalistic. Because the Carib people dominated the islands and the sea surrounding them when Europeans arrived, the area became known as the Caribbean.

By the 1400s, the Carib were concentrating their attacks on the larger islands of what today is known as the Greater Antilles. It has been estimated that between 30,000 and 75,000 Taíno lived on Borinquén, the island farthest east in the Greater Antilles. Though the Carib were better fighters, the Taíno were better organized and could call up more people to fight. Late in the century, however, a far greater threat sailed into the harbor on the northwestern tip of the island.

Puerto Ricans in costume for modern reenactment of a Taíno dance

Christopher Columbus

Cristoforo Colombo was born in Genoa, Italy, in 1451, the first son of Domenico Colombo, a weaver. "Christopher Columbus" is the English version of his Italian name. Columbus, hoping to become a sea captain, signed on as an ordinary seaman to get the experience he needed. A disastrous voyage landed him in Portugal, where he taught himself to read and to navigate at sea. While he was studying, he supported himself as a mapmaker for Portugal. In 1479, he married Felipa Perestrello Moniz, who gave birth to their son, Diego, in 1480.

Columbus found information that led him to believe that India and China could be reached by sailing west. He presented his idea to King John II of Portugal and asked for financing to prove it. When the king turned down the idea, Columbus went to King Ferdinand and Queen Isabella of Spain. He waited eight years, but in 1492, the royal couple agreed to finance his voyage.

After four attempts to find a western route to Asia, Columbus returned to Spain in 1504 in poor health and was labeled a failure. He never received recognition for having discovered new lands. Two years later, in 1506, he died in Valladolid, Spain, a broken man. ■

European Discoverers

Christopher Columbus, an Italian explorer sailing under a Spanish flag, landed on Borinquén in 1493. Columbus was looking for a faster, easier route to the riches of Asia. When Columbus reached the string of islands in the Caribbean, he named them the Antilles, from the Latin word *ante* meaning "before." He believed that the islands lay just "before or in front of" Asia.

During his first exploration of the area in 1492, he heard native stories about a large gold mine on the island of Hispaniola. Columbus left a colony of thirty-nine men on that island in a fort made from the wood of a damaged ship, the *Santa María*. Then he gathered gold trinkets, exotic animals, brightly colored parrots, native cloth—and some of the natives—to take back to Spain.

The *Niña* and the *Pinta* arrived in Palos, Spain, on March 15, 1493. The king and queen greeted Columbus and presented him

Columbus's three ships—the *Pinta*, the *Niña*, and the *Santa Maria*

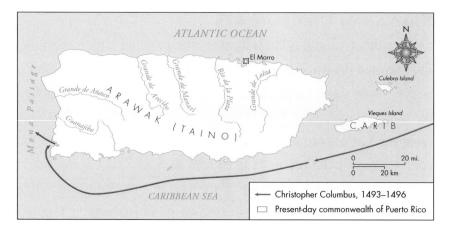

Exploration of
Puerto Rico

with all the honors and titles they had promised. Within months, he was on his way back to the Antilles, now referred to as the "West Indies" because he was sure he had reached India, to start more colonies and search for gold.

On Columbus's first trip, Ferdinand and Isabella had allowed him only three ships. On his second voyage, Columbus had seventeen ships and 1,500 men. Columbus's fleet also included mapmakers, priests, skilled craftsmen, and soldiers.

Columbus began his exploration around the southern islands of the Caribbean, today known as the Lesser Antilles, claiming all newly discovered lands for Spain. Making his way north toward Hispaniola, he and his men stopped on various islands to look for gold and lay claim to the land. On one island, a small group of natives made Columbus understand that they had been captured and carried away by the Carib and wanted to go home. Columbus agreed and took the natives with him on his way north. As they neared one large island, the natives jumped overboard and swam to their homeland—Borinquén.

Columbus sailed along the island's western coast into a bay where his ships took on fresh water, food, and other supplies. The date of the landing was November 19, 1493, but his exact landing place is not known.

Columbus named the island San Juan Bautista, or Saint John the Baptist, and then set sail for Hispaniola. San Juan Bautista was largely ignored until 1508, when Juan Ponce de León was given permission to create colonies in the West Indies.

der
nish Rule

The Spaniards realized that the island Columbus had named San Juan Bautista was not India. Though Columbus had failed to find vast treasures of gold or other precious metals, they believed that the West Indies might still be a source of wealth and power. Other Spanish explorers were then sent to the Caribbean to search for treasures, but the island of San Juan Bautista was largely ignored for the next ten years.

San Juan in its early days

Juan Ponce de León, who may have accompanied Columbus on his 1493 voyage, was governor of part of Hispaniola. Using that island as a base, he landed on the southern coast of San Juan Bautista in 1508. He traveled north to just south of San Juan Bay, where he founded a settlement called Caparra. The following year, having been named the first governor of San Juan Bautista, he began an intense search for gold. Some gold was found, but the source quickly ran out, along with Ponce de León's interest in the area.

When Ponce de León returned to Hispaniola, he was ordered by King Ferdinand to stop the constant raids by the Carib on San Juan Bautista. Caparra proved to be too far inland to support a military campaign at sea, so Ponce de León established a new base on the north side of San Juan Bay. It stood on a narrow piece of land that could be fortified against attack. The bay was a natural

Opposite: Spain's King Ferdinand VII

Juan Ponce de León

Juan Ponce de León was born in Tierra de Campos, near the town of Palencia in northern Spain, in 1460. Noble by birth, he served as a page in the Spanish court. Most historians believe he took part in Christopher Columbus's voyage to the West Indies in 1493, but some say he did not reach the Caribbean until 1502.

Ponce de León explored Puerto Rico, where he discovered some gold and became the first governor of the island in 1509. In 1512, King Ferdinand chose Ponce de León to lead an expedition to North America for conquest and settlement. He explored the Caribbean up to Florida, which he thought was an island. He named the land La Florida, the name it still holds. He returned to Spain and received permission to try to colonize Florida. In 1521, he was wounded in a battle with the Calusa Indians on that peninsula and died of his injuries a few days later in Cuba.

The popular story of Ponce de León's search for the Fountain of Youth is probably more myth than fact. Historians believe that even though Ponce de León had heard the tales of a Fountain of Youth, his real interests were in gaining wealth and power. ■

harbor, well protected from the storms of the Atlantic, and defensible against attack from the sea.

San Juan Bay became the center of Spanish exploration in the Caribbean. The explorers and traders who stopped there began to call it Puerto Rico. Over time, or perhaps through a mapmaker's error, the island and its capital switched names. The island became known as Puerto Rico and the "rich port" was called San Juan.

The Search for Profit

Profit was the main motivation for Spanish colonization in the Americas. To ensure that Spain would get all the benefits, its colonies were forbidden to trade with other countries. Once settlements were established, however, the Spanish kings thought the colonists should support themselves. This was not easy. Supplies from Spain arrived infrequently, as did payment for products shipped to Spain. Soldiers sent to guard the colonies were not paid regularly. The Spanish settlers in Puerto Rico bore a large financial burden.

They continued to hunt for gold and to mine what they found. As the limited gold veins were exhausted, the settlers started to take advantage of the climate to raise crops. Much of the wealth of Puerto Rico came from cultivated crops, such as sugar and coffee. To grow and harvest these crops with any hope of profit, Spanish landowners needed cheap labor. They found it in the Taíno people, whom they forced into slavery. Then, in 1513, the Spanish government allowed African slaves to be brought to the colonies to be used as labor.

Even with the increase in slave labor, it was hard to turn a profit in Puerto Rico. Hurricanes, epidemics of smallpox and yellow fever, constant attacks by the Carib, and the plundering of coastal towns by the French eventually drove most Spaniards off the island. Only the growing city of San Juan survived.

Attacks on San Juan

Puerto Rico proved disappointing as a source of profit, but the Spanish government found its location perfect for defending their

Destroying the Taíno

When Columbus arrived, 30,000 to 40,000 Taíno lived on the island. During the early years of colonization, the Spanish settlers made slaves of these people to provide the labor needed for farming. As the Taíno died of overwork and disease, their numbers declined rapidly, leaving the landowners of Puerto Rico with a labor shortage. By the end of the sixteenth century, few Taíno were left and the plantation owners began to depend on African slaves. ■

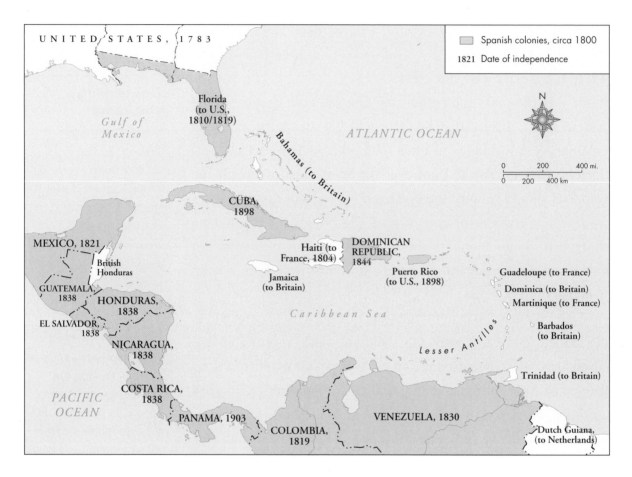

UNITED STATES, 1783

Florida (to U.S., 1810/1819)

Gulf of Mexico

Bahamas (to Britain)

ATLANTIC OCEAN

Spanish colonies, circa 1800

1821 Date of independence

N

0 200 400 mi.
0 200 400 km

CUBA, 1898

MEXICO, 1821

British Honduras

GUATEMALA, 1838

HONDURAS, 1838

EL SALVADOR, 1838

NICARAGUA, 1838

COSTA RICA, 1838

PACIFIC OCEAN

PANAMA, 1903

COLOMBIA, 1819

Haiti (to France, 1804)

Jamaica (to Britain)

DOMINICAN REPUBLIC, 1844

Puerto Rico (to U.S., 1898)

Caribbean Sea

Guadeloupe (to France)

Dominica (to Britain)

Martinique (to France)

Barbados (to Britain)

Lesser Antilles

Trinidad (to Britain)

VENEZUELA, 1830

Dutch Guiana, (to Netherlands)

Historical map of Puerto Rico

Caribbean and South American colonies. In 1532, Spain constructed La Fortaleza, a fortress near the shore at San Juan. Even before it was completed in 1540, however, it was found to be inadequate for the defense of the bay. In 1539, construction of a second fortress began. Named El Morro, the fortress stood at the entrance to the harbor. With both fortresses in place, San Juan was secure.

This security was challenged in 1585, when the English explorer Sir Francis Drake laid siege to the city. Intent on stealing the Spanish gold stored at La Fortaleza, Drake led twenty-seven ships and 4,500 men to capture San Juan. Warned of Drake's approach, Puerto Rico's governor, Pedro Suárez, blocked the bay

La Fortaleza was built as a fortress, but years later it was converted into the governor's mansion.

by sinking several Spanish ships. Unable to sail into the harbor, Drake anchored east of the city to put it under siege. But his ships were vulnerable to cannon fire from El Morro, and the English gave up and sailed away.

In 1598, another Englishman, George Clifford, the third earl of Cumberland, was more successful. Cumberland landed his forces on an undefended beach and marched overland to San Juan, avoiding the firepower from El Morro. He held the capital for more than five months before an epidemic among his troops forced him to

George Clifford, the third earl of Cumberland

abandon the island. He took everything of value, including slaves, crops, and church bells, and then burned down the city.

The Dutch sailed to San Juan in 1625 and laid siege to the city. They gave up after a month, but they also torched the city before they left. This incident led the Spanish to rebuild and fortify the entire city. A wall more than 22 feet (6.7 meters) high and more than 18 feet (5.5 m) thick was built around San Juan.

Spain's Fortress in the Caribbean

During the next century, colonists tried to make a living in agriculture. Spain never sent as many slaves as were needed, however, and by law, Puerto Rico could not trade with any other country. During some periods, no ships arrived in Puerto Rico at all, making it impossible for Puerto Ricans to earn a living.

In 1765, Spain realized that trade with its main defensive colony was almost nonexistent. The Spanish king sent Field Marshal Alejandro O'Reilly, an Irishman serving in the Spanish army, to look into the matter. O'Reilly discovered that the Spanish-appointed governor was a poor administrator, concerned primarily with his own pleasure and position. Laws were not enforced and corruption was widespread. Public roads and buildings were in need of repair. The only schools and hospitals were managed by the church. As O'Reilly had guessed, the island's economy was based on smuggling.

O'Reilly returned to Spain with a number of recommendations that gradually brought changes. The wall surrounding the city was completed and another fort, San Cristóbal, was built to strengthen its defenses.

The ruins of Fort San Cristóbal as they appeared in 1940

To shore up the economy, O'Reilly recommended that the sugar industry be revived. The timing was perfect. Just as the Puerto Rican sugar plantations began to produce, the American Revolution broke out, and sugar shipments to North America from British-held Jamaica and Barbados stopped. Puerto Rico gladly began sending its sugar north.

Finally, following O'Reilly's recommendations, the Spanish began to invest in Puerto Rico. But they were too late—just as the island was gaining some self-sufficiency, Spain was losing its position as a world power.

Spain Loses Its Empire

Spain had been a world power for nearly three centuries. Spanish troops had conquered most of Mexico, Central and South America, the Caribbean islands, and the Philippines. By the eighteenth century, however, Spain found itself in a contest with Britain for land and power in North America. During the American Revolutionary War (1775–1783), Spain sided with the colonies and declared war against Britain.

Soon the Spanish were embroiled in a war in Europe. Napoléon Bonaparte seized control of France in 1799. In 1808, Napoléon's French forces marched into Spain, forcing King Ferdinand VII to give up the Spanish throne. The Spanish people's fight to free themselves from France lasted until 1814.

The American Revolutionary War and the long war with France cost Spain all its overseas territory except a few outposts in Africa, the Philippines, Guam, Cuba, and Puerto Rico. Many of its possessions in South America declared independence while Spain was too busy to send troops to fight.

Spanish loyalists, fleeing the revolutionary fervor in Mexico and South America, made their way to Puerto Rico. The Spanish government was functioning in exile while King Ferdinand was held prisoner by Napoléon. In 1810, that government rewarded the loyalists and tried to satisfy Puerto Ricans by granting them a representative in Spain's *Cortes*, or legislature, in Madrid.

Lieutenant Ramón Power y Giralt was appointed to represent the island. Born in Puerto Rico to Spanish parents, Power was well educated and well traveled. In 1810, he sailed to Spain with a list of requests from the Puerto Rican people. They wanted support for education and public works, local elections, the removal of farming and trade restrictions, and a decrease in taxes.

Power got some of the reforms. In 1811, the Power Act was passed creating the Office of Intendency. The *intendente*, or public official, would be a civilian leader. The Cortes also approved opening more trade ports, eliminating some taxes and customs duties, and granting local governments greater power.

While serving in the Cortes, Power helped draft the Constitution of 1812. It granted Spanish colonists a set of civil rights similar to the Bill of Rights in the U.S. Constitution.

This new status did not last long, however. Power died of yellow fever in 1813. When Ferdinand VII regained the throne the following year, he scrapped the constitution and stripped Puerto Ricans of their rights. The Office of Intendency was untouched and Puerto Rico was still free to trade with other nations, however.

Governor Miguel de la Torre encouraged activities such as cockfighting.

The Revolutionary Spirit

For the next forty years, Puerto Rico suffered at the hands of a series of governor-dictators appointed by the Spanish rulers. These men—often called "little Caesars"—were charged with keeping Puerto Rico as a Spanish possession. The first of these repressive governors, Miguel de la Torre, set a 10:00 P.M. curfew. Later, he decided happy people were less likely to cause trouble, so he lifted the curfew and encouraged public entertainments, such as cockfighting and

Peasants lived in modest homes on small pieces of land.

horse racing. During this time, the government, fearing a slave uprising, passed the *código negro*, or black codes, which punished black people for the smallest slights against whites. Striking a white person was punishable by death.

Another governor-dictator, Juan de Pezuelas, required all agricultural workers to start carrying a *libreta*, or passbook, in 1849. Anyone found to be without this passbook, which described the person's work history, was sentenced to eight days of forced labor. Pezuelas also banned travel between cities, shut down the cockfight pits and racetracks, and required anyone who wanted to give a party to request official permission.

These restrictions helped feed the growing revolutionary spirit. The ability to trade with other nations did little to help raise the standard of living for most Puerto Ricans. Most of the cultivated land was owned by a small number of wealthy families, who had slaves to work for them. Between the wealthy few and the slaves— who made up about 10 percent of the population—were the many farmworkers. They toiled constantly to earn a bare living on their own small plots of land or as laborers on large plantations.

The spirit of revolution was also fed by a cholera epidemic that spread throughout the island in 1855. Thirty thousand people died of that infectious disease.

A physician named Ramón Emeterio Betances worked tirelessly throughout the epidemic. When it was over, he turned his energies to helping Puerto Rico's emerging revolutionary movement. He was joined in his efforts by Segundo Ruiz Belvis, Román Baldorioty de Castro, and José Julián Acosta. These men advocated reform of the Puerto Rican government, an end to slavery, and full civil rights for all Puerto Ricans. In 1862, Betances was jailed and then exiled.

While in exile in Paris and New York City, Betances formed the Puerto Rican Revolutionary Committee. The committee made plans to go to war, but the Spanish authorities discovered the plot. Rather than wait, committee leaders on the island chose to act. In 1868, in what came to be called *El Grito de Lares*, or "the Shout of Lares," several hundred men captured the mountain town of Lares. They proclaimed a new nation, the Republic of Puerto Rico. However, within days, government forces captured the rebels, putting an end to the new republic.

Betances failed in his attempt to make Puerto Rico independent, but he lived to see slavery abolished on the island. In 1873, after 350 years, slavery was abolished in Puerto Rico.

With problems at home, the Spanish government left Puerto Rico in the hands of another governor-dictator. In 1887, Governor Romualdo Palacios González tried to put an end to all revolutionary activity. Hundreds of people were arrested, and many died under torture. In the end, neither Palacios Gonzalez's efforts at repression nor his removal from power stopped the revolutionary movement on the island.

Mateo Práxedes Sagasta was head of Spain's Liberal Party during the late-nineteenth century.

Poverty in Puerto Rico had grown worse. Puerto Ricans were wondering whether life would be better if they governed their own island. Many people believed it was time to change Puerto Rico's political status.

The Autonomist Party was formed in 1882. Its members believed that Puerto Rico should be autonomous—govern itself—but keep its ties with Spain. To accomplish the goal of self-government, they decided to align themselves with Spain's Liberal Party. The Autonomist Party leader, Luis Muñoz Rivera, went to Spain in 1895. Mateo Práxedes Sagasta, Spain's Liberal Party leader, promised that Puerto Rico would be granted self-government if his party won

Luis Muñoz Rivera

Luis Muñoz Rivera, born in Barranquitas in 1859, was a newspaper editor and politician. He led the movement to obtain the Autonomic Charter from Spain in 1897. He was head of the newly organized Puerto Rican government for only a short time before the United States invaded the island during the Spanish-American War. He continued to seek autonomy for the island, working with the U.S. political system to gain self-government through the Foraker Act of 1900. Muñoz Rivera was appointed resident commissioner of Puerto Rico, the island's representative in Washington, D.C., and served until his death in 1916. His son, Luis Muñoz Marín, also took up the cause of Puerto Rican autonomy.

control of the Spanish government. When the Liberal Party came to power in 1897, it honored Sagasta's promise to the island.

Muñoz Rivera met with the Spanish parliament to plan the government of Puerto Rico. They wrote the Autonomic Charter of 1897, under which Spain would appoint the Puerto Rican governor-general, but the island would have both an elected assembly and representation in the Cortes in Spain. The charter went into effect in mid-July 1898, and eight days later, the United States invaded the island. Once again, Puerto Rico's status was in doubt.

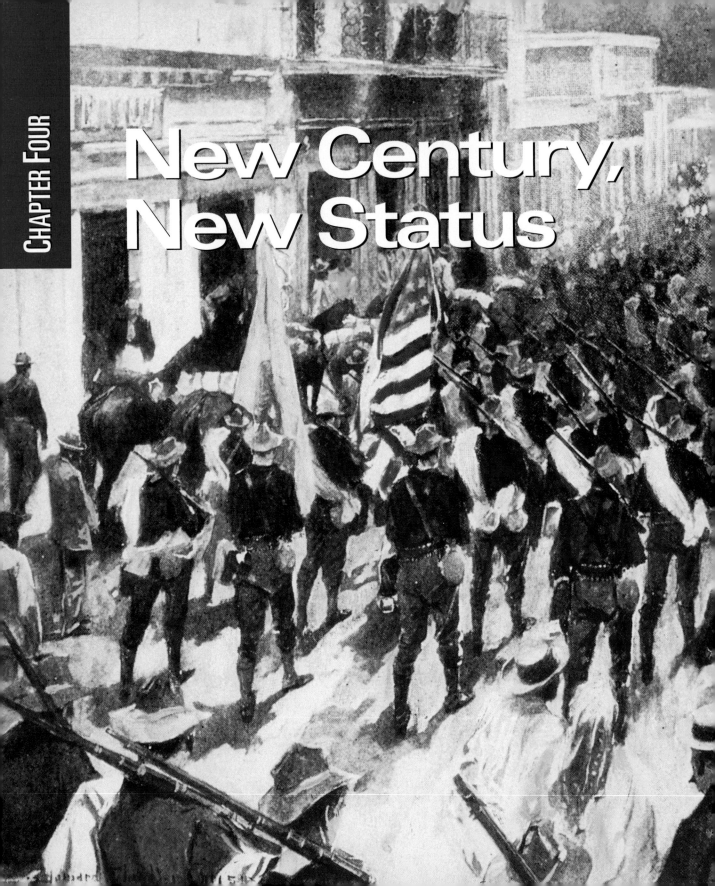

CHAPTER FOUR

New Century, New Status

U nited States armed forces landed at Guánica Bay on July 25, 1898, during the Spanish-American War. The war really had little to do with Puerto Rico. Instead, it concerned Cuba's revolution and an urge by the United States to kick Spain out of the "backyard" of the United States—the Caribbean. When the Spanish-American War ended on December 10, 1898, Puerto Rico, Cuba, and the Philippines came under the protection of the United States.

The U.S. cruiser *St. Paul* firing on the Spanish destroyer *Terror* off Puerto Rico in 1898

The U.S. military leaders who were assigned to establish a temporary government in Puerto Rico found the island's people in poverty. Most of the inhabitants were illiterate and poor, living in crude huts clustered in small villages. Ponce and San Juan vied for prominence as the island's leading city, but the other island towns simply struggled to exist. The island had only 175 miles (282 kilometers) of paved roads. Puerto Rico's income depended on the large tobacco and sugar plantation owners. More than 70 percent of the cultivated land was owned by 2 percent of the people. Almost everyone else worked for or in support of the plantations.

Opposite: U.S. troops entering Ponce during the Spanish-American War

The Puzzling Puerto Ricans

It was clear that something needed to be done, but the United States did not know how to deal with an already settled area. The U.S. government was accustomed to acquiring regions, such as Alaska and the Pacific Northwest. Few people lived in these areas and there was no preexisting government, organized religion, or established political groups.

Things were different in Puerto Rico. Nearly a million people lived on the island. A government was in place, and a religion was well established. Also, the people of the United States were mostly Anglo-Saxon Protestants who spoke English. The Puerto Ricans were Roman Catholics of Indian, African, and Spanish descent who spoke Spanish.

The question facing U.S. president William McKinley was how to proceed. He sent investigators to report on the condition of the island. A clergyman reported that the Puerto Rican people were "moral, industrious, intellectually able, obedient and respectful of law," but the military leaders in temporary charge had a different view. Brigadier General Guy V. Henry wrote to McKinley, "I understand that these people are anxious for another form of government. . . . They are still children. Each one has a different idea, and they don't really know what they want."

The general had probably based his opinion on his very recent knowledge of Puerto Rican politics, which then, as now, focused on the question of status. Luis Muñoz Rivera's political party wanted to gain the island's autonomy from Spain. When the United States acquired Puerto Rico, Muñoz Rivera worked toward the same goal with the United States.

Brigadier General Guy V. Henry reported to President McKinley about conditions in Puerto Rico.

Another Puerto Rican political leader, José Celso Barbosa, had worked with Muñoz Rivera to gain the Autonomic Charter from Spain, but he and his party wanted independence for the island. After the United States took control, a number of Puerto Ricans, including Barbosa, began to look forward to statehood.

Military Rule

The U.S. military view prevailed. The military's main interest in Puerto Rico was to hold it as a territory of, and fortress for, the United States in the Caribbean. The first order of business on the island was to establish English as the official language and make the U.S. dollar the official monetary unit.

Tobacco crops were an important part of Puerto Rico's economy.

For two years, the United States military governed the island, reminding Puerto Ricans of their years under the Spanish-appointed "little Caesars" who had governed the island in the early part of the nineteenth century. Once again, the appointed military governors controlled every aspect of Puerto Rican life. Local governments were dissolved, and newspapers were ordered to shut down. Every aspect of the island economy was under the control of the U.S. government.

At the urging of U.S. tobacco and sugar industries, a high tariff, or import tax, was placed on items from Puerto Rico to discourage North Americans from buying them.

Then a hurricane hit the island, killing more than 3,000 people and destroying the coffee crop and most of the trees. By 1900, the three major crops that had supported the Puerto Rican economy had disappeared or lost their main market.

A New Government

Military rule did not last long. In April 1900, Congress passed the Foraker Act, which called for a civilian governor to be appointed by the president of the United States. A legislature was established. The upper house was appointed by the president. The lower house was to be elected by the people.

However, only literate adult males who owned property were allowed to vote. Because 85 percent of the islanders were illiterate, and fewer still owned any land, most people could not vote and therefore did not have a voice in the governing process.

Although Puerto Ricans had a limited participation in government, the Foraker Act contained no provision for a path to statehood or any other form of self-rule. Originally, Senator Joseph Foraker had proposed that Puerto Ricans be granted U.S. citizenship, but this idea was thrown out. Muñoz Rivera wrote to President McKinley, saying that the Foraker Act was "unworthy of the United States which imposes it and of the Puerto Ricans who have to endure it."

In the military's view, Puerto Ricans were children who needed tutoring before they could govern themselves. Accordingly, the Americanization of Puerto Rico began. The first civil governor of Puerto Rico was Charles H. Allen.

The United States, unlike Spain, poured money and human

Puerto Rico experienced growth at the beginning of the twentieth century.

resources into Puerto Rico. Schools, roads, and dams were built, sanitation was improved, and during the first decade of the twentieth century, the island's economy increased 400 percent. After two years, the high U.S. tariffs on Puerto Rican sugar and tobacco were dropped.

Though the economy improved, working conditions did not. By this time, most of the large plantations on the island were run by U.S. companies. The plantation workers' wages were kept low to provide maximum profit for the owners. People who were poor under Spanish rule were still poor under the U.S. government.

Many Puerto Ricans believed this situation would not change until they were allowed to govern themselves. Once again, Luis Muñoz Rivera went to the island's ruling nation, asking for autonomy for Puerto Rico. This time he went to Washington, D.C., instead of Madrid.

Muñoz Rivera was Puerto Rico's congressional representative, or resident commissioner, from 1911 to 1916. In 1916, he argued before Congress in favor of home rule for the island. When some congressmen said Puerto Ricans were not educated enough for self-government, Muñoz Rivera pointed out that 80 percent of Americans could not read when the U.S. Constitution was signed. Congress ignored that though and voted down home rule. Muñoz Rivera died several months later, feeling he had failed his people.

President Woodrow Wilson signed the Jones Act into law.

War and Change

The year after Muñoz Rivera died, the Congress that could not be persuaded by common sense was moved by the force of war. German submarines fired on U.S. ships and sank them, bringing the United States into World War I.

In March 1917, President Woodrow Wilson signed the Jones Act into law. It allowed Puerto Rico to elect its own senate and some of the members of its cabinet. It also granted U.S. citizenship to the people of the island. With the rights of citizenship came the responsibilities, which included service in the armed forces. During World War I, 18,000 Puerto Rican men served in the U.S. Army.

There were flaws in the Jones Act. Puerto Ricans could make more decisions, but Washington was still the major power on the island. The president of the United States appointed the island's governor, many of its cabinet members, and its Supreme Court justices. Where military men had been governors under the Foraker Act, the Jones Act brought businessmen and politicians. These governors tended to see Puerto Rico as a permanent territory of the United States. They wanted to make life in Puerto Rico just like life in the United States, ignoring the uniqueness and validity of Puerto Rican culture.

The Jones Act also failed to deal with the fact that Puerto Rico had no middle class. It was still an island of peasants and millionaires, and working conditions for the poor were now worse than ever. Under the old plantation system, field workers were allowed a few acres in which to grow their own food and raise livestock. With U.S. business interests in charge of the plantations, workers were paid wages only. They had to buy everything else. Because most food, clothes, and other necessities were imported from the United States, prices were very high. People began to leave the fields and move into the cities, primarily San Juan, hoping to find better-paying jobs.

Once again, a hurricane blew through Puerto Rico. In 1928, a storm destroyed what little remained of the coffee and sugar plantations on the island. It killed hundreds of people and demolished hundreds of thousands of homes. With the island economy in ruins and the population growing by 40,000 people a year, Puerto Rico was not prepared for the worldwide slump in business of the 1930s—the Great Depression.

A Puerto Rican village in 1905

President Franklin Roosevelt's New Deal programs helped people in the United States make it through the depression, but it did little to help the Puerto Ricans. Free health clinics were established, and people were encouraged to grow their own food, but unemployment became worse. People were starving and something had to be done.

A Party for Independence

During these hard times, the Nationalist Party, led by Pedro Albizu Campos, began to rally Puerto Ricans to seek independence, sometimes using terrorism. Educated at Harvard University in Cambridge, Massachusetts, Albizu Campos felt Puerto Rico's future was with the other Caribbean nations instead of with the United States. In 1936, Nationalists staged a rally at the University of Puerto Rico. It turned into a riot and a number of people were killed. Albizu Campos and seven of his followers were arrested on charges of conspiracy to overthrow the United States in Puerto Rico. They were jailed in a federal prison in Atlanta, Georgia.

In March 1937, Puerto Rican nationalists asked permission to hold a parade in Ponce, located on the south side of the island. When the government refused to grant the permit, the Nationalists marched anyway, and police were called. A shot was fired, and police responded by shooting into the crowd. When the riot was over, 20 people were dead and more than 100 were wounded. Puerto Ricans remember March 21 as the day of the Ponce Massacre.

A Party for Autonomy

Luis Muñoz Marín, son of Luis Muñoz Rivera, knew both Washington, D.C., and Puerto Rico. He had favored independence for Puerto Rico but, by the late 1930s, he had decided that independence was not financially possible. Along with other advocates of self-government for the island, he formed the Popular Democratic Party in 1938. The party wanted autonomy for Puerto Rico and

El Jíbaro

El jíbaro symbolizes the folk hero of Puerto Rico. The idealized jíbaro lived a hard, independent life. Patient, hardworking, and honest, the jíbaro had a natural intelligence that enabled him to survive and take care of his family. His word was his bond. The jíbaro wore a wide-brimmed hat, known as a *pava*, a simple, rough shirt, and trousers. He is often pictured as carrying a machete for cutting through the forests, for farming, and for defense.

The image of the jíbaro was created in the eighteenth century. At that time, the rural people of Puerto Rico were called jíbaros. The origin of the name is uncertain, but it may have started during the Spanish colonial period. The jíbaros were of native island heritage (some were a mix of native island and African heritage). At the beginning of the twentieth century, the sugarcane plantations drew the jíbaros from the hills to work in the fields. ∎

help and support for the rural poor. It adopted a silhouette profile of the *jíbaro*, or traditional peasant, as its emblem. The party's slogan was *Pan, Tierra, y Libertad*, or "Bread, Land, and Liberty."

For two years, Muñoz Marín traveled throughout the rural interior of Puerto Rico gathering support. His work paid off in 1940 when the Popular Democratic Party gained enough votes in the Puerto Rican senate to make Muñoz Marín president of that legislative body.

By the time Muñoz Marín became a major political figure in Puerto Rico, the United States was fighting World War II. More than 65,000 Puerto Ricans served in the U.S. armed services during that war. The war helped the United States recover from the economic hard times of the depression. Luis Muñoz Marín, with the support of Franklin D. Roosevelt's appointed governor, Rexford Guy Tugwell, worked to bring Puerto Rico out of poverty.

Tugwell was unique as a federally appointed governor. Most governors knew little about Puerto Rico and did not even speak Spanish. Tugwell, however, hoped to do a good job as governor, benefiting Puerto Ricans. Unlike many previous governors, he consulted with the leaders of the Puerto Rican people before making important decisions. Together, they organized utilities that took running water and electricity to remote villages for the first time. He also helped poor farmers get land.

A Puerto Rican unit enjoying time off during World War II

Luis Muñoz Marín

Often referred to as "the father of modern Puerto Rico," Luis Muñoz Marín was born in San Juan in 1898. Like his father, he believed in Puerto Rico's right to self-government. They also believed the best way to achieve autonomy was through good government, rather than by revolution. Muñoz Marín was educated in the United States, where his father served as resident commissioner.

Like his father, Muñoz Marín began his career in journalism but soon became a political activist. In 1938, he helped found the Popular Democratic Party and was elected to serve as president of the Puerto Rican senate two years later. In 1949, he became the first elected governor of Puerto Rico, a position he held until 1965.

When the United Nations pushed the United States to define its relationship with Puerto Rico, Muñoz Marín helped devise the island's commonwealth status, which took effect in 1952. He also helped develop Operation Bootstrap, a program to help the island's economic recovery. After serving as governor for sixteen years, he declined another election and served in the Puerto Rican senate until his death in 1980. Muñoz Marín's daughter, Victoria Muñoz Mendoza, was a candidate for governor of the island in 1992. ◼

Commonwealth Status

Governor Tugwell's dedication to the island helped to change the United States–Puerto Rican relationship. In 1947, Congress passed the Butler-Crawford Bill, amending the Jones Act. The bill allowed Puerto Ricans to elect their own governor, who could in turn appoint his or her own cabinet. For the first time in their 400-year history, the Puerto Rican people elected their own head of government. A large majority voted for the Popular Democratic Party candidate, Luis Muñoz Marín.

Five years later, more positive changes came through Public Law 600, signed by President Harry Truman. Known as the Constitution Act, it granted Puerto Rico status as a commonwealth. A large part of the definition of commonwealth came as a result of Muñoz Marín's efforts to gain Puerto Rican autonomy. Muñoz Marín defined the new status as *estado libre asociado*, or "free associated state." The United States chose to call it a commonwealth, but both sides agreed on what the association would mean to the island. Puerto Ricans retained their U. S. citizenship, but they would not pay federal income taxes. They could vote for their own government officials, but they could not vote for the U.S. president. They also had no voting representative in Congress. The island would continue to use U.S. currency and postage. Now, however, Puerto Rico would have its own flag and anthem like any other sovereign nation.

The Constitution Act also brought federal aid for highways, housing, health, education, and other programs. In addition, Puerto Ricans became eligible for social security, unemployment insurance, and other federally funded social-welfare programs.

On July 25, 1952, coinciding with the fifty-fourth anniversary of the U.S. landing at Guánica Bay, Governor Muñoz Marín raised the new flag of Puerto Rico to an equal level with the Stars and Stripes flying over El Morro. This did not please everyone. Puerto Rican nationalists were outraged. While the commonwealth's constitution stabilized Puerto Rico's relation to the United States, it did not settle the question of status. There

In 1952, the Puerto Rican and United States flags were first flown at equal heights over El Morro.

The Shooting in the House

Fueled by nationalism, terrorist activities had been going on in Puerto Rico and the United States. They culminated on March 1, 1954, when three men and a woman entered the visitors' gallery of the U.S. House of Representatives in Washington, D.C., and opened fire on the representatives below. Five congressmen were wounded as the attackers shouted, "Puerto Rico is not free!" The attackers were arrested and sentenced to life in prison, though President Jimmy Carter released them many years later. ■

was still a strong nationalist movement on the island. Many supporters of independence for Puerto Rico felt that "commonwealth" was just another name for "colonialism."

Operation Bootstrap

Although Muñoz Marín was unable to settle the "status question" to everyone's satisfaction, he did make major changes in the economy and society of Puerto Rico. Through a series of government programs called Operation Bootstrap, Muñoz Marín rebuilt the island's economy from a reliance on agriculture to one that is based on industry. The program offered mainland businesses both federal and local tax exemptions. This, along with the lower wages of the Puerto Rican worker, lured U.S. companies to establish manufacturing operations on the island.

Muñoz Marín also worked to build Puerto Rican society. He established the goals of education, health care, and adequate housing for everyone. By the 1960s, Puerto Rico was a model for other Caribbean nations and much of South America, which were still struggling to recover from the poverty created by the worldwide depression.

After serving four terms as governor, during which he had dealt with four U.S. presidents, Muñoz Marín declined to run again. He wanted the Popular Democratic Party to develop new leadership. The party's candidate, Roberto Sánchez Vilella, won the 1964 election, but four years later the economy had changed and so had the will of the people.

Companies lured by this economic opportunity set up factories to produce clothing, pharmaceuticals, and electronics. Hoteliers were also drawn to Puerto Rico as part of the plan to expand the tourist trade.

A Party for Statehood

In 1967, Congress reacted to the many expressions of discontent by allowing the Puerto Rican people to cast their votes on the question of status, but it was a nonbinding vote—the United States would not be obligated to approve any changes in the island's status. The Nationalists boycotted the opinion poll, or plebiscite, although 65.9 percent of the registered voters participated. Of those who voted, more than 60 percent favored commonwealth, 39 percent voted for statehood, and less than 1 percent wanted independence.

Luis A. Ferré

The following year, the Partido Nuevo Progresista (PNP), or New Progressive Party, won the governor's race. Formed in 1967 to push for statehood in the plebiscite, the party's candidate was Luis A. Ferré, an industrialist. He reinforced the industrialization and Americanization of Puerto Rico. As a candidate, Ferré declared status was not an issue, but as soon as he became governor he began pushing for statehood. Both his stance on the question of status and an economic downturn caused the people to vote against Ferré and the New Progressive Party in the election of 1972.

The Status Question Continues

Since the middle of the twentieth century, Puerto Rican politics has been driven by the question of status. The Popular Democratic Party candidate, Rafael Hernández Colón, won the 1972 election. In 1976, the New Progressive Party candidate, Carlos Romero Barceló, was elected governor and he was reelected

Governor Pedro Rosselló, a strong supporter of statehood

in 1980. Colón was returned as governor in 1988. In 1992, New Progressive Party candidate Pedro Rosselló was elected governor. He was reelected in 1996.

These two political parties are still the main parties on the island, each with a major platform based on the status issue. The people's concern, however, is not with status but with economics and culture. Most Puerto Ricans—and many other U.S. citizens—believe Puerto Rico is better off economically tied to the United States. Many people also believe that a change to statehood would mean the cultural Americanization of Puerto Rico.

In 1993, another vote brought no change in status. With a large percentage of registered voters participating, 48.6 percent voted for commonwealth status, 46.3 percent favored statehood, and 4.4 percent continued to support independence. Less than 1 percent of the voters submitted blank ballots in protest of the uselessness of the nonbinding vote.

The 1993 vote was held while Governor Rosselló, a strong supporter of statehood, was in office. In 1998, Rosselló, thinking that some of the changes he instituted had moved Puerto Rico toward statehood, called for another vote. One of the changes was to sell a portion of the state-run telephone utility to an American communications company—an action that led to the first general strike by workers in many decades. This, along with the devastating hurricane Georges, kept Puerto Ricans unable to reconsider seriously the question of status. The governor campaigned hard for statehood, but once again, the opinion vote failed to bring a change in status.

The 1998 vote was different in one important way. There were five options on the ballot: statehood, independence, current commonwealth status, somewhat freer commonwealth status, and "none of the above." With a voter turnout of more than 73 percent, a majority of Puerto Ricans voted for "none of the above." The voting was: statehood, 46.49 percent; current commonwealth status, 0.06 percent; independence, 2.54 percent; changed commonwealth status, 0.6 percent; and none of the above, 50.3 percent.

Politicians and news commentators interpreted the results in several ways. Some said the voters were confused about the two different versions of commonwealth status. Some said the people were voting for the status quo. And others believed the vote was a clear message to the governor that the people were not yet ready to revisit the issue of status. Governor Rosselló promised to continue to fight for statehood. Whatever the interpretation of the plebiscite, it is clear that Puerto Rico's status is still a question waiting for an answer.

In 1999, the governor pointed out that Puerto Rico can be regarded as the oldest colony on Earth. He asked the Decolonization Committee of the United Nations to list Puerto Rico as a "non–self-governing territory" and to insist that the United States clarify its status in 2000.

Rafael Hernández Colón

CHAPTER FIVE

A Tropical Island

P uerto Rico is an island in the West Indies set in the Caribbean Sea. The West Indies is an archipelago, or chain of islands, which marks the boundary between the Caribbean Sea and the Atlantic Ocean. This chain of islands stretches in a great curve from the tip of Florida to the coast of Venezuela in South America.

Three island groups make up the West Indies—the Bahamas, the Greater Antilles, and the Lesser Antilles. The Bahamas, the northernmost islands, lie closest to the United States. The Lesser Antilles, the southernmost smaller islands, are closest to Venezuela. The Greater Antilles, in the middle of this island chain, include Cuba, Jamaica, Hispaniola, and Puerto Rico.

The easternmost island of the Greater Antilles, Puerto Rico is about 1,000 miles (1,609 km) south of Florida. It is a tropical island with mild temperatures and exotic plants and animals. Life

Puerto Rico is known as a tropical paradise.

Opposite: The Caribbean National Forest

on the island has adapted to sunny days with short bursts of rain and little temperature variation. The average temperature range is from 73° Fahrenheit (23° Celsius) in January to 80°F (27°C) in July. Frost never forms and snow never falls, but rain is a constant. In some parts of the island, rain falls almost every day. These daily showers usually do not last long, however. The northern coast gets more rain than the south and is cooler. The southwest part of the island is warmer and drier. El Yunque, a mountain in the Caribbean National Forest at the eastern end of the island, gets the most rain.

The word "hurricane" comes from the Taíno word *huracán,* which is derived from the name of the Taíno god of evil winds. Hurricane season in Puerto Rico lasts from June through November. These tropical storms hit the island, on average, once every ten years. Although hurricanes are dangerous and very destructive, Puerto Rico has an early warning system today that alerts the people of the island days in advance.

Culebra, one of Puerto Rico's island dependencies

Puerto Rico has a roughly rectangular shape. It is about 3,515 square miles (9,104 square kilometers) in area. This area includes the three largest islands that Puerto Rico governs, which are Vieques and Culebra to the east and Mona to the west. Vieques, the largest of the three, is used for military maneuvers by the U.S. Navy. Culebra, which lies to the northeast across Vieques Passage, is designated a National Wildlife refuge. Mona, a seabird sanctuary in the center of Mona Passage, lies between Hispaniola and Puerto Rico. Several other small dots of land, called cays or keys, are also considered part of Puerto Rico.

Mountains, Hills, and Valleys

Hills and mountains cover about three-fourths of the island. There are four main land regions—the coastal lowlands, the coastal valleys, the foothills, and the central mountains.

The coastal lowlands border the north and south coasts of the island. The northern lowlands are 8 to 12 miles (13 to 19 km) wide with a generally humid climate. Most of Puerto Rico's popular beaches are located on its northern coast. The island's capital and largest city, San Juan, stands here. The southern lowlands are drier and cover a narrower area that rises abruptly to rugged mountain peaks. Ponce, the third-largest city in Puerto Rico, is in the southern lowlands. Sugarcane is an important crop in both areas.

Extending inland from the coast on the east and west are the coastal valleys. Most of this land is used for raising sugarcane. Coconuts and other fruits also grow in these areas.

The foothills rise in long chains running east and west, just inland from the northern and southern coastal lowlands. Much of the area consists of jagged peaks and rounded basins. The basins formed when water wore away the limestone under the hills, causing the ground to sink. This process, known as karstification, has resulted in one of the most extensive cave systems in the Western Hemisphere, a honeycomb of caves throughout the island.

Running east and west across the south-central part of the

island is the central mountains region. The main range is the Cordillera Central. The highest peak in Puerto Rico, Cerro de Punta, 4,389 feet (1,339 m), stands in this range. A secondary range is the Sierra de Luquillo. The mountain region also has many fertile valleys where farmers raise coffee and citrus crops.

Cordillera Central in the central mountains region

Rivers, Lakes, and Streams

There are fifty-seven rivers in Puerto Rico. The longest, such as Río Grande de Arecibo, flow north from the mountains into the Atlantic. The swiftest are those in the north, tumbling down the Cordillera Central mountain range, sometimes disappearing into underground caves and then reappearing as spectacular waterfalls.

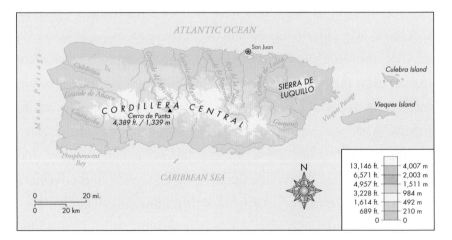

Puerto Rico's topography

Puerto Rico's Geographical Features

Total area	3,515 sq. mi. (9,104 sq km), including Vieques, Culebra, and Mona Islands
Land area	3,459 sq. mi. (8,959 sq km)
Inland water area	56 sq. mi. (145 sq km)
Coastline	311 miles (500 km)
Tidal shoreline	700 miles (1,126 km), including bays and inlets
Highest point	Cerro de Punta, 4,389 feet (1,339 m)
Lowest point	Sea level along the Atlantic Ocean
Largest city	San Juan
Population	3,808,610 (2000 census)
Record high temperature	103°F (39°C) at San Lorenzo on August 22, 1906
Record low temperature	40°F (4°C) at Aibonito on March 9, 1911
Average July temperature	80°F (27°C)
Average January temperature	73°F (23°C)
Average annual precipitation	70 inches (178 cm) in the north; 37 inches (94 cm) in the south

One of these rivers is the Río La Plata, or the Plata River, which runs 46 miles (74 km) from about Cayey on the southern side of the Cordillera Central to Dorado on the northern coast. Other rivers on the island include the Río Grande de Bayamón, the Río Grande de Loíza, and the Río Grande de Manati. Puerto Rico's rivers are not deep enough to carry oceangoing ships, but they are important for irrigating fields and generating hydroelectric power.

There are few natural lakes or ponds on the island. During the twentieth century, sixteen artificial lakes were created to collect irrigation water for the island's agriculture. Many of these lakes were stocked with game fish to provide recreational fishing for local residents, as well as tourists.

There are 1,200 streams running throughout the island, both on the surface and through the honeycomb of caves they helped create in the limestone rock. Many of the streams are slow-moving bodies that empty into a series of brackish inlets and lagoons that lace the island's coast. The largest of these inlets is San Juan Bay, a natural harbor on the Atlantic coast.

San Juan Bay

An Island of Trees

Puerto Rico was once filled with natural vegetation. Away from the coastline, a large part of the island was forest. Most of the interior of the island was rain forest. Today, much of the island's forestland has disappeared. All that remains of Puerto Rico's rain forest is in the Sierra de Luquillo mountain range in the northeast. It surrounds El Yunque Peak, in the Caribbean National Forest, the largest of the island's nature preserves with 27,890 acres (11,295 hectares). A number of smaller forest preserves are found throughout the island.

More than 3,300 species of trees and plants grow in Puerto Rico. Some of these trees and plants are found nowhere else. One of the most important of the 547 native species of trees is the ceiba, or silk-cotton tree. It grows to an enormous size and lives for more than 300 years.

Impatiens growing in the El Yunque rain forest

Papayas are not native to Puerto Rico.

Rain forest trees often produce the hardest woods known, which is one reason so many of them have been cut down. In the past, Puerto Rican forests produced valuable ebony and sandalwood trees. The densest wood in the world comes from Puerto Rico's guayacán tree. It is so heavy it sinks in water. Another hardwood tree is the rare and much prized ausubo tree. Its wood is so hard it can chip an ax. Today, when old houses are torn down, the ausubo beams are saved for restoration projects.

Trees that have been introduced into Puerto Rico and have flourished include Dominican mahogany, used in furniture making, and Indo-Malayan coconut palm, papayas, mango, and tamarind. The Spanish colonists brought citrus trees.

Much of Puerto Rico's forestland has been cut down for commercial use. Today, the island must rely on imports for lumber, paper, and pulp by-products. In an effort to reforest the island, the Puerto Rican government has planted fast-growing trees such as eucalyptus, teak, and Honduran pine. If the reforestation succeeds, Puerto Rico will one day grow enough trees to supply all its own lumber needs.

Flowers add color and beauty to island vegetation. Many of these flowers grow on trees, such as the white flowers of the indio tree, the blue flowers of the guayacan, and the yellow flowers of the campeche. Ornamental vines and shrubs add to the floral array.

These flowering plants include bougainvillea, carallita, jasmine, hibiscus, orchids, gardenia, poinciana, and poinsettia.

Bougainvillea is among the island's flowering plants.

Along with its rain forests and seacoasts, Puerto Rico has drier areas where succulent plants such as cacti are found. These, too, produce colorful flowers. The barrel-shaped Turk's cap cactus produces red flowers, the prickly pear has yellow blossoms, and the squat melon cactus produces pink flowers and fruit. Another dry-climate plant is called the century plant. Its thick, spiky leaves grow in a rosette at the base with tall flower stalks rising out of the center. According to the myth that gave it its name, the plant blooms only once in a hundred years. Actually, it blooms at twenty years of age and then dies. Its fiber is mixed with cotton to make hammocks and mats. Aloe, a plant with sap that soothes burns, cuts, and rough skin, also grows in Puerto Rico's drier regions.

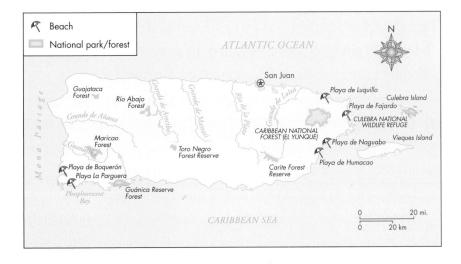

Puerto Rico's parks and forests

Puerto Rico's Animals

Though indigenous island plant life is abundant, mammals are rare. Cows, pigs, mongeese, and horses were Spanish imports. In fact, with the exception of bats, dolphins, and manatees, Puerto Rico has no native mammals. Manatees are huge, clumsy-looking sea cows found in coastal rivers. Puerto Rico's manatees, like those in Florida, are threatened.

Puerto Rico is famed for a horse called the Paso Fino. Described as the horse of the Spanish conquistadores, it has a unique gait that makes riding it "as smooth as glass." There are more than 7,000 of these smooth-walking horses on the island, and they are being bred elsewhere in the world.

A not-so-prized mammal is the mongoose. Originally imported to keep down rats and poisonous reptiles, these small animals have multiplied into an agricultural pest.

Culebra Island's giant leatherback turtles are at the opposite end of the size scale. Black with narrow fins, the leatherbacks are so named because, instead of hard shells, they have leatherlike hide. This species of reptile grows up to 7.5 feet (2.3 m) long and weighs up to 1,200 pounds (545 kilograms). In danger of extinction, it is officially protected, but its main enemies are humans.

Other island reptiles include green turtles, anole lizards, iguanas living on Mona, and snakes. Thanks to the mongeese, there are no poisonous snakes on Puerto Rico, but there is at least one dangerous one. The Puerto Rican boa can grow to 7 feet (2 m) long and is capable of crushing the life out of most mammals.

Puerto Rico has perhaps 200 species of birds. These include the Puerto Rican grackle, several species of owls, whippoorwill, woodpecker, and grosbeak. The two species of hawk are the Puerto Rican sharp-shin and the West Indian red-tail. Birds living along the coast include ducks, sandpipers, terns, and plovers.

At least two bird species are in serious trouble. The Puerto Rican parrot is about 12 inches (30 centimeters) long with bright green feathers. It was nearly wiped out when much of El Yunque's rain forest was cut down. Even after careful protection, fewer than 100 birds exist today. The Puerto Rican nightjar, also on the island's endangered species list, is nearly invisible because its dark brown coloring allows it to hide in dense foliage.

Puerto Rican sharp-shins

As might be expected of a tropical island, marine life in and around Puerto Rico is mostly of the oceanic variety. Fish living in the waters around the island include barracuda, herring, marlin, mullet, pompano, sharks, snappers, Spanish mackerel, and tuna. Lobsters, crabs, shrimp, and oysters are also found in Puerto Rican waters.

With its beautiful beaches, the island seems to beckon people to wade in the water or walk on the beach. The life-forms hiding in these places include sea urchins, sea cucumbers, starfish, jellyfish, and the Portuguese man-of-war. Watch out, though, because some of these sea creatures sting!

Starfish can be found along Puerto Rico's shores.

CHAPTER SIX

Places Old and New

The main port for Puerto Ricans traveling to North America and
for the island's many visitors is San Juan, the capital of this beautiful island. This city has many faces, as do its people, the
Sanjuaneros, who make up more than 10 percent of the island's
population.

San Juan is a modern capital city, the center of the island's government. It also has a major business district, where the lifestyle is
modern and fast-paced. Here, high-rise office buildings house
local, regional, and national companies. In Old San Juan, the pace
is a bit slower and the entire area is a living monument to Puerto
Rico's fascinating past.

**Old San Juan's town
wall and harbor**

Old San Juan

The original settlement of the city now called San Juan took place
in 1521 on the curved spit of land protecting San Juan Harbor.
This area was enclosed in a wall to protect the Spanish colonists.

**Opposite: Plaza de
Armas in San Juan**

Touring El Morro

Fuerte San Felipe Del Morro, known simply as El Morro, is the smaller of the two forts that stand guard over Old San Juan. El Morro's entrance is at the end of a park, formerly a drill square. The fort sits on 74 acres (30 ha) and its 18-foot (5.5-m)-thick walls rise 140 feet (42.7 m) above the sea. Rounded sentry boxes, known as *garitas*, stand at intervals along the walls. They are unique to Puerto Rican forts and serve as the official symbol of the island.

To the right of the fort entrance is a ramp leading to the Port of San Juan Lighthouse, which marks the channel entrance to San Juan Harbor. Inside the fort is a small museum. A steep, triangular staircase leads to the gun emplacements. ■

Within the wall is El Morro, the fort that stands guard over San Juan Bay.

By the middle of the twentieth century, Old San Juan had deteriorated badly as the city's active life took place in other areas. Seven blocks of the old downtown area were declared a historic district in 1949. The next year, the United States designated it a national historic zone. The Institute of Puerto Rican Culture soon began a massive restoration of the old city. The institute's work was rewarded when Old San Juan was declared a UN World Heritage site.

More than 400 sites have been restored in Old San Juan and many of the restored buildings are now museums. The streets are narrow and paved with cobbles of adoquine, a blue stone cast from unburned furnace waste. Four plazas and two forts are among the historic sites. Two of the plazas honor Christopher Columbus, Ponce de León is honored in another, and the fourth was planned as the main city square. The two forts are El Morro and San Cristóbal. El Morro was built to protect against invasion from the sea, while San Cristóbal was built to ward off land attacks. Both forts are national historic sites.

Other points of interest in Old San Juan are Casa Blanca, or "White House," the residence built by Ponce de Léon; El Convento Dominicano, a Dominican convent built on land donated by Ponce de Léon; and Iglesia de San José, the oldest church still in use in the Americas. For 350 years, this church held Ponce de Léon's tomb, until it was moved to the city's cathedral.

Museo de las Américas, built to house Spanish troops, is now a cultural arts museum for the Americas. Museo de Casals is

The Dominican convent in Old San Juan

dedicated to cellist Pablo Casals. Centro Nacional de Artes Populares y Artesanías (Popular Arts and Crafts Center) consists of an art gallery and shops where the island's best folk art and works by contemporary artists are on display.

Visitors to Old San Juan are entertained with year-round festivals. Many of these colorful holidays celebrate saints, the seasons, and the arts. Other festivals celebrate music. There are two jazz festivals, one in May and one in June. The Casals Festival of classical music and the Latin Music Festival are also held in June.

San Juan and Its Districts

Puerta de Tierra is the seat of Puerto Rican government today. This small area of San Juan, which lies just outside the old walls, was first settled by freed black slaves. El Capitolio, Puerto Rico's capitol, sits in the middle of this district. Built between 1925 and 1929, the building is a white classic-style structure similar to the White

San Juan along the Condado Lagoon

House in Washington, D.C. The Archives and General Library of Puerto Rico are also here. Unusual for a public library, there is a small chapel on the first floor. The last major construction project of the old Spanish government, this building was originally built as a hospital in 1877.

East of Puerta de Tierra is Santurce, once considered the heart of the San Juan area. Businesses have deserted this deteriorating area for the newer business district in Hato Rey. Centro de Bellas Artes is the home of a thriving arts community. The government has designated $400 million to restore the area.

The Hato Rey district of San Juan is the Wall Street of the Caribbean, the banking and financial center for the island nations surrounding Puerto Rico. Called the *Milla de Oro*, or "Golden Mile," this district has high-rise buildings that house the offices of major corporations and businesses with internationally recognized names, such as Citibank and Unisys. There are also government offices in this district.

The botanical gardens at the Agricultural Experimental Station

Just south of Hato Rey, in the section called Río Piedras, is the University of Puerto Rico. Nearby, Luis Muñoz Marín's home is now restored as a museum, and visitors love to shop at the Paseo de Diego, the largest pedestrian market in San Juan. The botanical gardens at the Agricultural Experimental Station are located south of the university. When completed, the gardens will be among the most extensive gardens of their type in the world, covering 200 acres (81 ha).

Eastern Puerto Rico

East of San Juan is Carolina, the site of the Roberto Clemente Sports City. It is dedicated to baseball great Roberto Clemente, who played for the Pittsburgh Pirates. Carolina is also home to many of the more than 100 manufacturers of medicines operating in Puerto Rico. This suburb of San Juan also has a large shopping mall called Plaza Carolina.

The main plaza at Loíza Aldea

A fishing village called Boca de Cangrejos, or "Point of the Crabs," lies farther east. Here, bird-watchers catch sight of terns, herons, sandpipers, and other feathered coastal inhabitants. Some of the best food on the island is served out of the picturesque shacks and food kiosks along the village beachfront. This beach is a favorite of sunbathers and surfers. Ice-cold coconut milk served in its shell is a favorite refreshment of the sun-and-surf crowd.

Only 6 miles (9.7 km) from metropolitan San Juan is Loíza Aldea, a predominantly African-American community. It is separated from its neighbors by a dense mangrove swamp and a massive woodland called Torrecilla Baja. The only way to Loíza is a very rutted road that crosses Río Grande de Loíza, Puerto Rico's only navigable river. Settled in the sixteenth century by African slaves sent to mine gold for Spain, the village is probably the purest center of African culture in the Western world. African culture is most visible during the Fiesta de Santiago Apóstol. Beginning on July 25, the celebration for Saint James lasts a full week. The Loíza Carnaval is a bit like Carnaval in South America or Mardi Gras in New Orleans, but the costuming is definitely African, similar to that worn by the Yoruba tribe of West Africa.

Farther down the coast is Luquillo, a popular white-sand resort area. Here the beachfront food stands are modern and numbered, but they serve many of the Puerto Rican favorites found in Boca de Cangrejos. Located near one of Puerto Rico's major mountain chains, Sierra de Luquillo, the town is known for its world-class surfing site—La Pared.

Fajardo, also on the east coast, has a double identity. It is a busy dockside town that serves as the gateway to the islands of Vieques and Culebra, and it is also a yachting community. Many of the yacht owners live in the condominiums built just north of town in Playa Sardinera, a fishing village. Marinas along the oceanfront between Fajardo and Playa Sardinera are crowded with large yachts and motorboats. Small seafood restaurants are a major attraction here.

Across the Vieques Passage from Fajardo lie the islands of Vieques and Culebra. Although politically connected to Puerto Rico, the two small islands are geographically part of the Virgin

Islands. Both Vieques and Culebra attract tourists looking for a laid-back island vacation spot. These islands can be reached by airplane from San Juan or by boat from Fajardo.

Vieques is the larger of the two islands. The beach at Esperanza, a small fishing village, is lined with guest cottages and restaurants. At beaches and bays around the edges of the island, visitors can enjoy snorkeling, diving, and swimming as well as sunbathing. The western end of the island is a U.S. Navy base.

Culebra, or Pirates' Cay, is a national wildlife refuge. President Theodore Roosevelt's last executive order established the refuge in 1909. Administered by the U.S. Fish and Wildlife Service, the island is the nesting place for a dozen species of marine birds. One of Culebra's best spots is Flamenco Beach where the sand is white, the water is clear blue, and, because it is a bit hard to get to, the beach is uncrowded. Nearby, a subtropical coral reef hides a species of sea lizard.

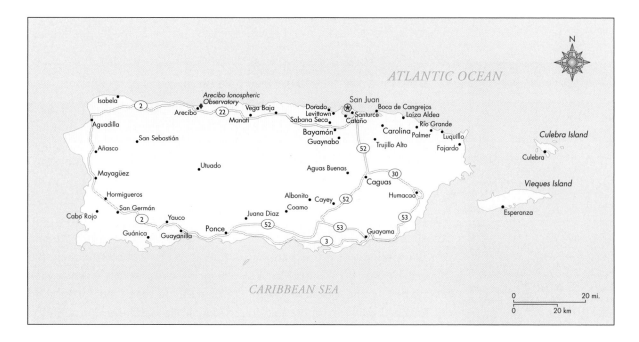

Map labels:

ATLANTIC OCEAN

Isabela
Arecibo Ionospheric Observatory
Aguadilla
Arecibo
(2)
(22)
Vega Baja
Manati
Dorado
Levittown
Sabana Seca
San Juan
Santurce
Cataño
Boca de Cangrejos
Loíza Aldea
San Sebastián
Añasco
Bayamón
Guaynabo
Carolina
Palmer
Río Grande
Luquillo
Culebra Island
Utuado
(52)
Trujillo Alto
Fajardo
Culebra
Mayagüez
Aguas Buenas
(30)
Vieques Island
Hormigueros
San Germán
Caguas
Humacao
Esperanza
Cabo Rojo
(2)
Yauco
Albonito
Coamo
Cayey
(52)
Juana Diaz
Guánica
Guayanilla
Ponce
(52)
(53)
Guayama
(53)
(3)

CARIBBEAN SEA

N

0   20 mi.
0   20 km

Puerto Rico's cities and major highways

Back on Puerto Rico the only tropical rain forest in the U.S. National Park System lies inland and west of Fajardo. Though it is listed as the Caribbean National Forest, the whole forest is widely known as El Yunque, after its most famous peak.

Southeast of El Yunque lies the town of Ceiba, home of Roosevelt Roads Naval Station. This naval base is the headquarters of the U.S. Caribbean Naval Forces and the base for the annual exercises of the fleet of the North Atlantic Treaty Organization (NATO).

Southwest of El Yunque is Caguas, named for Caguax, a Taíno Indian leader. The largest town in the island's interior, it is set in the fertile Turabo Valley. Caguas is a modern city with a European flavor. In Plaza Palmer, the heart of the city, a statue of favorite son José Gautier Benitez, a nineteenth-century poet, overlooks two huge rubber trees with benches built into their trunks. The Cathedral de Caguas faces the city hall across the square.

Visiting El Yunque

The Caribbean National Forest is 27,890 acres (11,295 ha) of tropical forest located 25 miles (40 km) southeast of San Juan. *El Yunque* is the Spanish word for "anvil." Viewed from the north, the second-largest mountain in the forest resembles an anvil.

The mountains in this national forest belong to Puerto Rico's Sierra de Luquillo mountain range. El Toro is the highest mountain in the park, rising 3,532 feet (1,077 m) over the forest. El Yunque, at 3,496 feet (1,066 m), is the second highest.

The entrance to the park is at Palmer, east of San Juan. South of Palmer is Route 191, which is now closed. This route went all the way through the park until the 1970s when a landslide blocked the road. A portion of that road is now a popular bicycle route through the rain forest. With Route 191 closed, the park is less accessible by car, so the best way to reach this forest is on foot. Trails lead hikers through the various forests and ecosystems, past spectacular waterfalls and a number of lookout towers with amazing views of the park. ■

Southern Puerto Rico

Between Caguas and Cayey is Aguas Buenas, known for the nearby network of caves. Tours of the caves were stopped when it was discovered that the caves were the source of a serious respiratory disease. The caves are still accessible, but only experienced spelunkers using air-filtering devices should explore them.

Cayey is one of the larger cities in Puerto Rico. It is a modern city with a number of large industries and a University of Puerto Rico campus. The art museum on this campus displays works by major Puerto Rican artists. The AT&T stations carrying most of the island's long-distance communications tower over the city from atop Sierra de Cayey mountain. Founded in 1773, Cayey was once

Exploring a cave near
Aguas Buenas

a coffee and cigar-producing center. Consolidated Cigars remains
one of the large manufacturers in the city.

Farther west is Coamo, the site of Coamo Springs. Even before
the Spanish discovered it, the Taíno people used the waters from the
springs for religious rituals and healing. Coamo Springs was once
a celebrated Caribbean resort where President Franklin D. Roosevelt came to take advantage of the healing waters in the 1930s.
The old resort went bankrupt after World War II, but a new one was
built on its ruins.

One of the oldest cities in Puerto Rico, Coamo was founded in
1579. A museum on the plaza holds 450 years' worth of artifacts.
The building was once the mansion of the town's wealthiest citizen,
Clotilde Santiago, a plantation owner and businessman. The church
on the plaza contains paintings by two of Puerto Rico's best-known

artists, José Campeche, who recorded many scenes of Puerto Rican life in the 1700s, and Francisco Oller y Cestero, who painted two centuries later.

The city of Ponce stands in the middle of Puerto Rico's south coast. The third-largest city on the island, Ponce is a port city on a natural bay. It has the best weather of all the island's cities, because it is located in what ecologists call a "rain shadow." The Cordillera

Many consider Ponce to be Puerto Rico's prettiest city.

Central mountains shield Ponce from the afternoon rains that fall all over the rest of the island.

Named after Juan Ponce de León y Loíza, the great-grandson of Puerto Rico's first governor, Juan Ponce de Léon, the city's architecture makes it the most Spanish of the island's cities. A beautification program by former governor Rafael Hernández Colón in the 1980s has given the city the reputation of being the prettiest on the island.

Ponce's historic district has two plazas, a number of historic museums, and several art galleries. Among these are the Ponce History Museum built to celebrate the 300th anniversary of the city; the Pancho Coimbre Museum commemorating Puerto Rico's famous baseball player; the Puerto Rican Music Museum; and Teatro La Perla, a 100-year-old theater and cultural center. The best known of the city's museums—the Ponce Museum of Art—houses the finest collection of European art in the Caribbean.

Festivals take place almost year-round in Ponce. In November, a heritage festival called *Descubre tus Raíces*, or "Discovering Your Heritage," is celebrated at Tibes Indian Ceremonial Center in a suburb of Ponce. The patron saint festival of Our Lady of Guadalupe takes place in December. A regional craft fair is held in late February or early March. The week before Ash Wednesday is Carnaval, a celebration similar to Mardi Gras. Ponce celebrates the *Fiestas de Cruz*, or "Festivals of the Cross," and a dance festival called Fiesta Nacional de la Danza in May.

West of Ponce is Guánica, the site of the 1898 U.S. invasion of then Spanish-held Puerto Rico during the Spanish-American War.

The Guánica Forest
Reserve

In addition to its history, Guánica is part of the Guánica Forest Reserve, home to all of Puerto Rico's bird species. The reserve is known for its cactus-scrub—subtropical dry forest—and was designated a Biosphere Reserve by the United Nations in 1975.

Bioluminescent Bays

A unique nighttime experience awaits visitors to the waters off the southwestern coast of Puerto Rico. Phosphorescent Bay is home to billions of microscopic marine creatures that flash a biological glow when their watery home is disturbed. Mosquito Bay on the southwestern coast of Vieques Island is also home to these bioluminescent organisms. ■

Western Puerto Rico

One of Puerto Rico's most popular tourist destinations is San Germán in the southwest part of the island. The second-oldest city in Puerto Rico, San Germán is unique among the island's tourist cities because it is not located on the coast. It is, however, the most historic town on the island. Founded in 1573 by Spanish colonists, the city once rivaled San Juan in importance. In the nineteenth century, it was surrounded by coffee plantations. San Germán resisted the urge to transform itself into a modern metropolis and became a living history museum.

Porta Coeli is an example of San Germán's historical importance. Founded in 1606, it is the oldest church under the U.S. flag and one of only a handful of Gothic churches in the Western world. Interesting historical artifacts can be found in the coffee barons' haciendas and the art museum called Museo de Arte y Casa de Estudio.

In the center of the island's west coast is Mayagüez. This industrial port city has a library, a zoo, and several museums. Also, an agricultural research station is located next to the Mayagüez branch of the University of Puerto Rico. The city's main industries are tuna-packing and pharmaceutical manufacturing. Founded at the end of the eighteenth century, Mayagüez's history under Spanish rule was almost totally lost in 1918 when an earthquake rocked the western part of the island.

Mona Island lies 50 miles (80 km) west of Mayagüez. Mona is the least known and least visited of all Puerto Rico's offshore

Mona Island is surrounded by coral reefs.

islands. The terrain is rocky and the foliage dense, giving shelter to rock iguanas and wild descendants of the bulls, boars, and goats kept by long-vanished pirates. A number of bird species find good nesting on Mona. The little island is surrounded by coral reefs.

Aguadilla is a small tourist town on the northwest tip of the island, not far from where Christopher Columbus first set foot in the Americas. Aguadilla and its neighbor Aguada have a long-running rivalry over which is the spot where Columbus first landed. Aguadilla is famous for its lace, music, and history. Immigrants from Belgium, Holland, and Spain brought the craft of *mundillo*. The finely embroidered lace produced by this craft is the pride of Aguadilla. In October, the town presents the Rafael Hernández Festival in honor of this world-famous composer. Historic places include Fort Concepción and Punta Borinquén Lighthouse. The

Arecibo Observatory

Arecibo Observatory, built in 1960, is so big that it can be seen from a jumbo jet flying at 30,000 feet (9,150 m). The dish, or curved reflecting surface, of the radio telescope is the largest in the world. It is suspended over a natural sinkhole in the limestone of the island and covers 20 acres (8.1 ha) with 40,000 perforated aluminum-mesh panels that form a dish 1,000 feet (305 m) in diameter. A 600-ton receiving and transmitting device is suspended 450 feet (137 m) over the dish to collect radio signals bounced up from the dish. Usually, dishes for radio telescopes can be moved to fine-tune reception. At Arecibo, the dish is immobile, but the receiver can be moved. A steel rim was added around the edge of the dish in 1993 to block out radio interference from other transmitting equipment on the island.

This observatory is credited with a number of astronomical discoveries. In 1992, the telescope helped to discover planets outside our solar system. In 1993, two U.S. astronomers used the observatory in the research that won them the Nobel Prize in physics. NASA also used the telescope extensively in their Search for Extra-Terrestrial Intelligence (SETI) program. The University of California at Berkeley now funds the SETI program. The huge dish "starred" in the movie *Contact,* based on Carl Sagan's novel. ▨

lighthouse has been designated a historic site by the National Register of Historic Places. Ramey Air Force Base, once a U.S. military installation, is now a visitors' center and receives flights from New York and Miami.

Northern Puerto Rico

On the northwest coast of Puerto Rico stands Arecibo, one of the oldest Puerto Rican towns. Founded in the sixteenth century, Arecibo is now the world's largest producer of pharmaceuticals. Another large employer in the city is Ronrico Rum. Plaza Luis Muñoz Rivera honors the hero and politician who played a major part in the history of Puerto Rico in the twentieth century.

The ruins of Caparra

The area's main attraction is the Arecibo Observatory, south of the city. Built with grant money from the National Science Foundation, the day-to-day operations of the huge radio telescope are managed by Cornell University of Ithaca, New York. It has a full-time staff of more than 100 people and hosts visiting scientists from all over the world.

Our circular tour of Puerto Rico leads back to San Juan's western suburbs, Bayamón and Cataño. The second-largest city in Puerto Rico, Bayamón was founded in 1509 as Caparra. It is now an interesting mix of old plantation buildings and modern architecture. Things to see in Bayamón include the ruins of Caparra, the Luis A. Ferré Science Park, and the Juan Ramón Loubriel Baseball Stadium. There is also the Oller Art and History Museum, named after the artist Francisco Oller, who came from Bayamón.

Just across San Juan Bay from the capital city is Cataño. The city's main attraction is the Bacardi Rum plant. Riding the Cataño ferry to San Juan offers a spectacular view of the bay and Old San Juan.

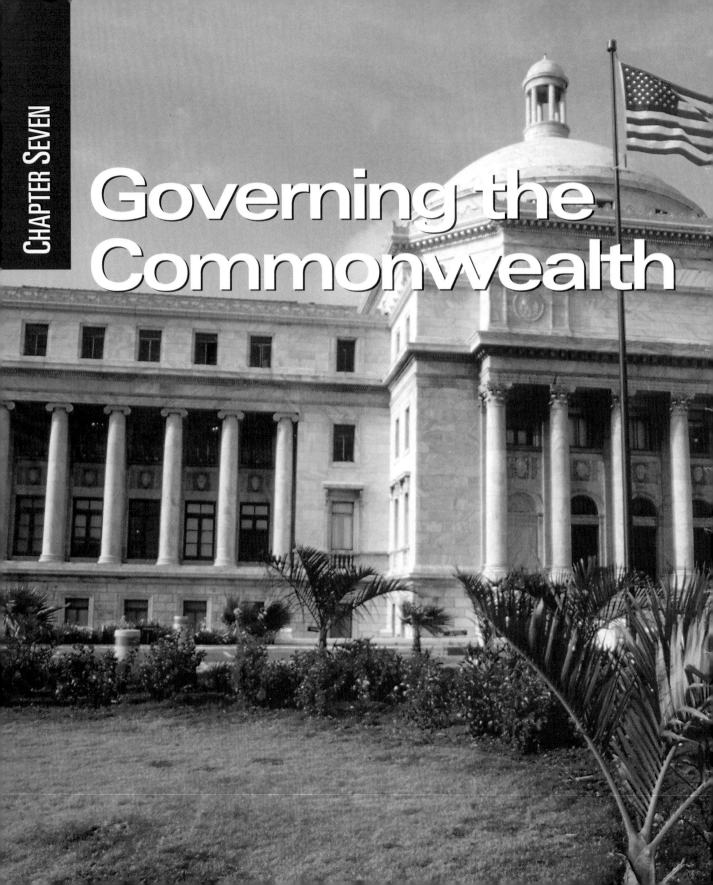

CHAPTER SEVEN

Governing the Commonwealth

City hall in Old San Juan

Because of its status as a commonwealth, Puerto Rico has a unique system of government within the political structure of the United States. The people of Puerto Rico are citizens of the United States, but they do not have all the rights and obligations of citizenship. Residents of Puerto Rico may not vote in presidential elections. They do not pay federal taxes. They do, however, serve in the U.S. military. Puerto Ricans who move to the mainland may vote and must pay taxes.

Puerto Ricans elect a resident commissioner to the U.S. House of Representatives. This individual, who serves a four-year term, may vote in committees of the House of Representatives but may not vote on final legislation.

Puerto Rico is governed by its own constitution, which was ratified on March 3, 1952. This constitution, modeled on the U.S. Constitution, set up a republican form of government and includes a bill of rights. Like the U.S. government, Puerto Rico's governing system is divided into three branches. The legislative branch makes the laws, the judicial branch interprets them, and the executive branch enforces them.

Opposite: The capitol in San Juan

Carlos Romero Barceló

Carlos Romero Barceló has held most of the major political posts in Puerto Rico. He was the first former governor to serve as Puerto Rico's resident commissioner in Washington, D.C. Born in Santurce, Romero Barceló was first elected mayor of San Juan in 1968. Reelected in 1972, he became the first Puerto Rican to be elected president of the National League of Cities, an organization of mayors of U.S. cities. Elected governor of Puerto Rico in 1976, Romero Barceló concentrated on the island's economy. He was reelected governor in 1980, then became resident commissioner in 1992. Romero Barceló holds a bachelor's degree in political science and economics from Yale University and a law degree from the University of Puerto Rico. ∎

The Executive Branch

The governor is elected by Puerto Rican voters to serve a four-year term, although he or she may be reelected an unlimited number of times. Candidates for governor must be citizens of the United States, have resided in Puerto Rico for at least five years prior to running for office, and be at least thirty-five years of age. The governor may approve or veto (refuse to approve) laws passed by the legislature, call special sessions of the legislature, proclaim martial law when public safety is threatened, and grant pardons. The governor also serves as commander in chief of the armed forces. Puerto Rico has no lieutenant

Aerial view of the governor's mansion

Puerto Rico's Governors

Name	Party	Term	Name	Party	Term
Jesús T. Piñero	Appointed	1945–1949	Carlos Romero Barceló	New Progressive	1977–1985
Luis Muñoz Marín	Popular Democratic	1949–1965	Rafael Hernández Colón	Popular Democratic	1985–1993
Roberto Sánchez Vilella	Popular Democratic	1965–1969	Pedro Rosselló	New Progressive	1993–2001
Luis A. Ferré	New Progressive	1969–1973	Sila M. Calderón	Popular Democratic	2001–
Rafael Hernández Colón	Popular Democratic	1973–1977			

governor, so a governor who dies in office is succeeded by the secretary of state.

With the approval of the legislature, the governor appoints justices for the supreme court, as well as many government department heads, known as secretaries. These secretaries function as an advisory council, or cabinet, known as the Council of Secretaries, to the governor.

The Legislative Branch

The Puerto Rican legislature is bicameral (two-house), consisting of a senate and a house of representatives. Members of both houses serve four-year terms. A candidate for the legislature must be a U.S. citizen, literate in Spanish or English, and be at least thirty years of age.

There are eight senatorial districts. Voters in each district elect two senators. All voters also elect eleven senators-at-large, meaning that it does not matter where the candidates

The legislature building

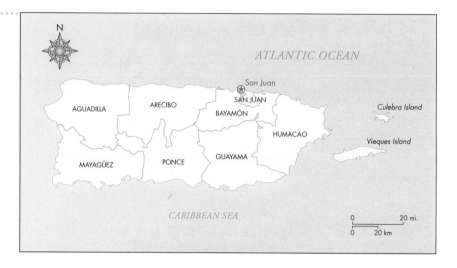

Puerto Rico's districts

live. There are forty legislative districts with one representative elected from each. Voters also elect eleven more representatives-at-large to represent all the commonwealth.

If one political party controls more than two-thirds of the seats of either house, the minority parties are allowed to elect extra senators or representatives-at-large. If no single party holds a two-thirds majority, the senate has twenty-seven senators and the house has fifty-one representatives.

The Judicial Branch

Puerto Rico's supreme court, the highest court in the commonwealth, holds its sessions in San Juan. A chief justice and six associate justices preside over this court. Supreme court justices may serve until the age of seventy.

Lower courts include the circuit court of appeals, the superior court, which is the major trial court in the commonwealth, and district and municipal courts, which hear cases on the local level. The governor appoints the thirty-three judges of the appeals court, and each judge serves a term of sixteen years. All judges are appointed by the governor, with the advice and consent of the senate. The 151 superior court judges are appointed to twelve-year terms. There are 58 district court judges appointed to eight-year terms and 105 municipal judges appointed to five-year terms. Federal cases are heard in the U.S. District Court for Puerto Rico. The seven judges of this court are appointed by the U.S. president.

Local Governments

Puerto Rico is divided into seventy-eight municipalities, or *municipios*. Many municipalities are cities, while others are centered on a small town and include rural areas. Voters in each municipality elect a mayor and an assembly. The mayor appoints a secretary-auditor and a treasurer. These officials make the laws that govern the municipalities.

Puerto Rico's Government

Executive Branch

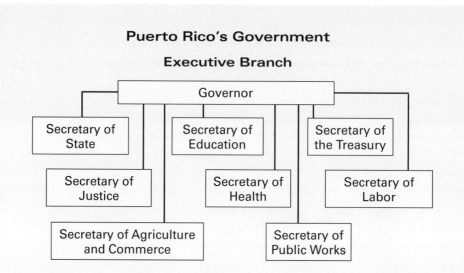

Governor

Secretary of State

Secretary of Education

Secretary of the Treasury

Secretary of Justice

Secretary of Health

Secretary of Labor

Secretary of Agriculture and Commerce

Secretary of Public Works

Legislative Branch

House of Representatives   Senate

Judicial Branch

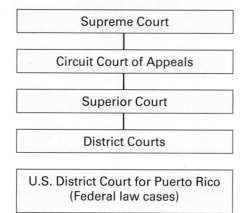

Supreme Court

Circuit Court of Appeals

Superior Court

District Courts

U.S. District Court for Puerto Rico
(Federal law cases)

José Celso Barbosa

Born in Bayamón in 1857, José Celso Barbosa is known as the father of the statehood for Puerto Rico movement. At the end of the Spanish-American War, he officially formed the pro-statehood Republican Party on July 4, 1899. Celso Barbosa was a physician and the first African-American person to attend Puerto Rico's prestigious Jesuit Seminary. In 1907, he established *El Tiempo* newspaper. He was elected to the Puerto Rican senate and held his senate seat until his death in 1921. ■

Politics

The major political parties were established based on the issue of Puerto Rico's political status, which continues to be a major issue. The two largest are the New Progressive Party and the Popular Democratic Party. The New Progressive Party platform is to make Puerto Rico a state in the United States. The Popular Democratic Party wants the island to continue as a commonwealth. A third party, the Puerto Rican Independence Party, favors complete independence for Puerto Rico. Four other political groups also participate in island politics. Political parties receiving at least 5 percent of the vote cast in elections receive financial aid from a government fund.

A Puerto Rican Independence Party rally in 1993

Puerto Rico's Flag and Seal

Puerto Rico's flag has five alternating horizontal bands of red and white. A blue triangle with a white star in the center extends into the stripes. Designed around 1895, it was officially adopted in 1952.

The Puerto Rican seal, or coat-of-arms, is an ancient one. Granted to Puerto Rico by Spain's King Ferdinand in 1511, it shows a lamb supporting a cross. The lamb symbolizes peace and brotherhood.

The *F* and *I* in the seal stand for King Ferdinand and his queen, Isabella. ■

Puerto Rico's Symbols

Puerto Rico's flower: Puerto Rican hibiscus, or *flor de maga* This large, showy flower thrives in Puerto Rico's warm climate. It has five petals and several pistils.

Puerto Rico's bird: Stripe-headed tanager, or *reinita mora* This colorful tropical bird feeds on fruit. Flocks eat all the fruit off one tree and then move on to the next.

Puerto Rico's tree: Silk-cotton tree, or *ceiba* This tree, also known as kapok, has bell-shaped flowers. The lightweight fiber from its fruits is used as stuffing in pillows and furniture.

Puerto Rico's animal: Coquí This tiny Puerto Rican tree frog (left) is found almost nowhere else in the world. This small creature grows no more than 1.5 inches (3.8 cm) high and has nearly transparent skin that allows it to blend with its background. Its charm is its song. Only the males of a few species sing—and then only during the evening hours. The two-toned song sounds as if the little frog is calling its own name—*koo-kee*.

Puerto Rico's Anthem
"La Borinqueña"

Lyrics by Manuel Fernández Juncoz
Music by Félix Astol y Artes

(Spanish)	(English)
La tierra de Borinquén	The island of Borinquén
Donde he nacido yo	Where I was born
Es un jardín florido	Is a tropical garden
De mágico primor	Of magic splendor.
Un cielo siempre nítido	A sky that is always bright
Le sirve de dosel	It's like an enchanted canopy
Y dan arrullos plácidos	And sing pleasant lullabies
Las olas a sus pies	The waves on your feet.
Cuando a sus playas llegó Colón	When Columbus arrived
Exclamó lleno de admiracion	Filled with admiration, he exclaimed:
Oh! Oh! Oh!	Oh! Oh! Oh!
Esta es la linda tierra	This is the beautiful land
Que busco yo	I'm looking for
Es Borinquén la hija	It's Borinquén, the daughter
La hija del mar y el sol	The daughter of the sea and sun
Del mar y el sol	The sea and sun
Del mar y el sol	The sea and sun

CHAPTER EIGHT

Puerto Rico at Work

Large plantations, growing sugar, coffee, or tobacco, supported the Puerto Rican economy in the nineteenth century. Today, the service industry provides close to 75 percent of the gross domestic product (GDP). The GDP is the total value of all goods and services produced within a region in a year. Farming produces only about 1 percent of Puerto Rico's GDP, but it remains important for many people.

A cattle ranch outside the town of Humacao

Farming and Fishing

About 60 percent of Puerto Rico's total land area is dedicated to farming. Unfortunately, the land has been overfarmed for hundreds of years, and now, in order to be productive, it must be heavily fertilized. In addition, fields in the drier southern part of the island and along the northwest coast must be irrigated.

In general, commercial crops are grown in the western half of the island. Coffee, the main commercial crop, is grown in the western part of the central mountain region. The coffee-growing industry employs about one-third of Puerto Rico's farmworkers. Commercial fruit crops include bananas, mangoes, pineapples, coconuts, and avocados, as well as oranges and other citrus fruit.

Food crops are grown primarily in the western half of the island. The main food products are plantains, beef, veal, pork,

Opposite: Harvesting coffee beans

eggs, fish, and mangoes. Despite all these crops, most agricultural income comes from milk, poultry, and eggs. As city populations grow, Puerto Rican farmers are increasing their livestock production.

Puerto Rico's annual fish catch amounts to about 8 million pounds (3.6 million kg) of fish and shellfish. Valued at about $16 million, a large portion of the catch is tuna and lobster, with lobster bringing in the most money.

Manufacturing

Puerto Rico has one of the most dynamic economies in the Caribbean. Key to this economic success was the island's rapid transition from agriculture to manufacturing and commerce. The transition began in the 1940s when Luis Muñoz Marín, with the aid of the federal government, began Operation Bootstrap. This program encouraged mainland manufacturers to establish operations in Puerto Rico and to earn important tax benefits in return. In the 1990s, these tax advantages were canceled. More than 100 factories closed, but many were so firmly established that they no longer required the tax benefits.

Goods manufactured in Puerto Rico include chemicals (such as pharmaceuticals), food products, electrical equipment, machinery, medical and scientific instruments, and clothing. The manufacturing of pharmaceuticals is the most important industry on the island. There are about 100 drug companies with plants producing pharmaceuticals for markets around the world. These companies also manufacture health-care products, such as intravenous solutions, blood-pressure kits, and thermometers.

Computer assembly is one of the island's manufacturing industries.

Other Puerto Rican manufacturing includes rubber and plastic products; stone, clay, and glass products; fabricated metals; leather and leather products; and tobacco products. Puerto Rico is also the world's largest producer of rum, an alcoholic beverage distilled from sugarcane. More than half of the rum is exported in bulk to the United States for bottling.

What Puerto Rico Grows, Manufactures, and Mines

Agriculture	Manufacturing	Mining
Beef cattle	Clothing	Clays
Coffee	Electrical machinery and	Lime
Milk	equipment	Salt
Poultry and eggs	Medicines	Sand and gravel
Sugarcane	Nonelectrical machinery	Stone
	Processed foods	
	Scientific instruments	

A salt mine in
Cabo Rojo

Mining

In a sense, one might say that Puerto Rico's most important mineral is the sand on its beautiful beaches. Otherwise, Puerto Rico's most valuable minerals are stone, sand and gravel, and lime. They are mined around the areas of San Juan and Ponce. Other minerals include clays and salt. Salt is mined (extracted) from seawater. At the start of the twenty-first century, SUNOCO, Inc., was expanding its oil refinery at Yabucoa.

Energy, Transportation, and Communication

The Puerto Rico Electric Power Authority (PREPA) produces electricity for the island. Created in 1941 as a public corporation, PREPA produces electricity through oil-fueled power plants. All oil is imported, making the public utility dependent on foreign oil producers. The only other sources of electric power are the small hydroelectric plants built by the United States in the early part of the twentieth century.

The island has about 14,612 miles (23,511 km) of mostly paved roads. The roads provide islandwide transportation for automobile, bus, and truck traffic.

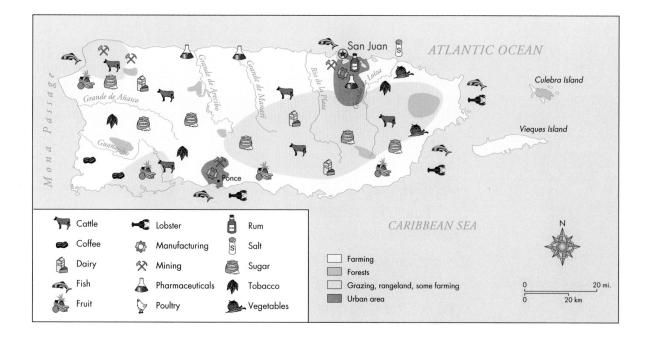

Legend

Cattle	Lobster	Rum
Coffee	Manufacturing	Salt
Dairy	Mining	Sugar
Fish	Pharmaceuticals	Tobacco
Fruit	Poultry	Vegetables

Farming
Forests
Grazing, rangeland, some farming
Urban area

0   20 mi.
0   20 km

Opening in 2002 will be the Tren Urbano, or "urban train," built on a budget of $1.4 billion. An aboveground light-rail system, it will serve the metropolitan area of San Juan, Bayamón, Santurce, Hato Rey, and Río Piedras. It is planned eventually to reach the airports at Isla Verde, Caguas, and Old San Juan.

Transportation to the island requires either a boat or airplane ride. The three main seaports are San Juan in the north, Ponce in the south, and Mayagüez in the west. San Juan, of course, is the busiest port. It is also the site of the island's main airport, Luis Muñoz Marín International.

Communications operations on the island include telephone, television, radio, newspapers, and the Internet. The telephone system

Puerto Rico's natural resources

San Juan Harbor

is operated by a government and business partnership. It is a modern system integrated with the U.S. systems by high-capacity submarine cable and through satellite with high-speed data capabilities. The islandwide system has about a million lines. Cellular service is also offered. Long-distance service goes through the submarine cable to the United States or direct from a satellite.

Puerto Rico is wired to the world through a number of Internet services. GTE offers Internet programming and E-mail services. America Online and Microsoft's Internet services are also available. E-programming is provided in Spanish and English. The Puerto Rican government's home pages are in both Spanish and English, but most information about essential programs and services are in Spanish.

A radio station in San Juan began broadcasting in 1922. The same station, WKAQ, also built the first television station, in 1954. Many Puerto Rican households have cable television service, which is, for the most part, broadcast in English.

A number of newspapers are published in Puerto Rico. *El Dia,* founded in Ponce in 1909 and the first islandwide newspaper, is no longer published. *El Nuevo Dia* is published in San Juan and owned by Luis A. Ferré Enterprises. Other newspapers published in San Juan are *El Vocero* and the *San Juan Star.*

Trade and Finance

The larger cities on the island have shopping malls with retail shops and restaurants familiar to Americans from the mainland. J. C. Penney's, Burger King, and the Gap can all be found in the larger cities. These stores are just a part of Puerto Rico's wholesale

and retail trade, which accounts for 14 percent of GDP and employs some 20 percent of the island's workers.

Fox Delicias Mall in Ponce

Other stores and restaurants across the island are of distinctly local origin. According to many travel guides, the best food is found in restaurants and roadside stands that are owned and operated by Puerto Ricans. The best shopping areas are the plazas de mercado (shopping plazas) in large metropolitan areas and towns.

Hato Rey, east of San Juan, is home to the island's financial district, the Golden Mile. Here banks, insurance companies, real estate companies, and international corporate offices operate in high-rise buildings along a section of Muñoz Rivera Expressway. Financial markets account for 13 percent of the GDP.

Financial district of
Hato Rey, known as
the Golden Mile

Banco Popular de Puerto Rico, located on the Golden Mile, is the oldest bank on the island. Founded in 1893, it is the banking and financial center of the Caribbean, where $8 billion in profits from Operation Bootstrap is on deposit. In the 1990s, Banco Popular began opening branches in major mainland cities.

Touting Tourism

Part of Operation Bootstrap's effort to modernize the Puerto Rican economy was directed at the tourist trade. Advertised on

the mainland as the most exotic location to visit without a passport, Puerto Rico draws more than $2 billion from tourism each year. Tourism accounts for about 6 percent of the GDP and employs about 60,000 people. Hotel industry wages average around $7.50 an hour.

Since 1985, more than $500 million has been invested to support tourism. A renewed ad campaign produced a 60 percent increase in visitors. As a result, hotel capacity increased from 8,500 to 12,000 rooms by early in the twenty-first century.

Many tourists are drawn to the island's luxurious resorts.

CHAPTER NINE

The Puerto Ricans

Visitors to Puerto Rico often see the island as a tropical paradise. Many of the island's poets and musicians have celebrated its beauty and the loving hearts of its people. The lyrics of "Mi Tierra Borincana," written by José Manuel Rivera, are an example of this sentiment: "How beautiful it is, to live in this dreamland! And how beautiful it is to be the master of the coquí's song!"

Feeding pigeons in
Old San Juan

Puerto Rico's paradise, however, is crowded today. The 2000 census counted 3,808,610 Puerto Rican residents. Puerto Rico has a population density of 1,101 people per square mile (425 per sq km). This gives each resident only about 0.5 acres (0.2 ha). The average population density in the United States is about 76 people per square mile (29 sq km).

Ethnic Heritage

Everyone in Puerto Rico is from somewhere else. Native peoples arrived first. They came to the island from South America in prehistoric times. The Spanish found paradise in the late 1400s, eventually calling it Puerto Rico. The Africans were brought by the

Opposite: Fishermen
with their catch

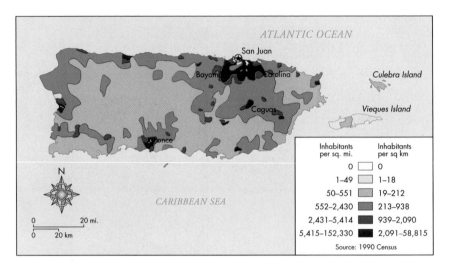

Puerto Rico's population density

Inhabitants per sq. mi.		Inhabitants per sq km	
0		0	
1–49		1–18	
50–551		19–212	
552–2,430		213–938	
2,431–5,414		939–2,090	
5,415–152,330		2,091–58,815	

Source: 1990 Census

Population of Puerto Rico's Major Cities (2000)

San Juan	434,374
Bayamón	224,044
Ponce	186,475
Carolina	186,076
Caguas	140,502
Arecibo	100,131
Mayagüez	98,434

Spanish as slaves beginning in the 1500s. The North Americans were the last to arrive, waiting until U.S. armed forces landed at Guánica in 1898 before sending large numbers of people to the island.

Although they are proud to be citizens of the United States, Puerto Ricans are not hyphenated Americans. They do not call themselves Puerto Rican–Americans. In fact, they do not refer to themselves as Americans at all. They are proud to be, and to call themselves, Puerto Ricans.

Neither do they separate themselves by ethnic background. It would be hard to do so. The ethnic heritage of the people is a mix of native peoples, African, Spanish, and some northern European, thanks to the adventurous pirates of the sixteenth and seventeenth centuries. Most Puerto Ricans are descended, in part, from Spanish colonists.

More often than other colonists of the Western Hemisphere, the Spanish intermarried with people of other races, such as island natives and the Africans brought as slaves. During the nineteenth

century, people from all over the world began to arrive. The Chinese came to build roads. Italians and Lebanese came to build communities. All of them stayed and were assimilated into the island society. In the twentieth century, North and South Americans also found their way to the island. Some North Americans came to do business and South Americans wanted to escape civil wars in their countries. All who stayed became patriotic Puerto Ricans.

The official languages of the island are Spanish and English. Business is conducted in both languages, but most of the island's government services are conducted in Spanish. Only about one-fourth of the people speak English.

The Puerto Rican people are descended primarily from Spanish colonists.

The Catholic Church
has a strong presence
in Puerto Rico.

Because of its Spanish heritage, Puerto Rico used to be predominantly Roman Catholic. Since the island became affiliated with the United States, Protestant faiths have grown. About 58 percent of the people are now Protestant. In recent years, evangelical fundamentalism has become popular.

Education

Education is a high priority in Puerto Rico. When the U.S. troops landed on the island in 1898, only 23 percent of the people could read and write. Today, the literacy rate is almost 90 percent. Children are required to attend school between the ages of five and seventeen. There are three levels of schooling. The primary level includes kindergarten plus six grades and the middle and high levels each have three grades.

Education for all children began in Puerto Rico when the United States took over the government from the Spanish. Puerto Rico's department of education administers the island's school system. The federal government provides large sums of money for education on the island. All federal laws governing education on the mainland also apply to Puerto Rico's schools.

The U.S. government required schools to teach in English until 1942, when the Puerto Ricans succeeded in changing that rule. Today, classes are taught in Spanish, but students study English as a second language for all twelve years of their schooling. About

José de Diego

José de Diego, born in Aguadilla on April 16, 1866, was a prominent Autonomist politician, poet, and orator. After the U.S. invasion in 1898, he tried to organize an armed resistance but soon turned to political means to gain independence. He was cofounder, with Luis Muñoz Rivera, of the Unionist Party in 1904. His dream was to establish a confederation of Spanish-speaking islands in the Caribbean. He also led the fight to have school courses taught in Spanish so that the language would not be lost. Considered the father of modern Puerto Rican poetry, one of his major works was *Cantos de Rebeldía*, or *Songs of Rebellion*. He died in New York City in 1918. ■

The University of Puerto Rico's main campus in San Juan

642,000 students attend public schools on the island. Another 120,000 are enrolled in parochial schools.

A large number of Puerto Rico's high school graduates go on to college. There are more than sixty-nine public and private institutions of higher learning on the island. Among these, the University of Puerto Rico, founded in 1903, is the largest. The university's main campus is in Río Piedras, just south of San Juan. Other campuses are located in Bayamón, Carolina, Ponce, Ramey, Arecibo, Mayagüez, San Juan, Cayey, and Humacao. The university also has a school of dentistry and tropical medicine in Old San Juan and a college of agriculture in Mayagüez.

The largest private university is Interamericana. It has eleven campuses throughout the island, with the main one being at San Germán, where it started.

Dining in Paradise

Life in the paradise known as Puerto Rico has different meanings to different people. For some, the fast-paced living of the financial district in Hato Rey offers the best lifestyle. Others prefer the beachcombing life of Boca de Cagrejos, within driving distance of San Juan. For those who live to shop, the plazas de mercado located throughout the island represent paradise. The boating life is found in Fajardo, the arts flourish in Ponce, and people in Arecibo are often caught stargazing.

Whatever their life-style or pace, Puerto Ricans take time to enjoy their food. It reflects the ethnic mix of the people themselves.

Fresh produce and many other items are sold at outdoor markets.

Casual dining in Old San Juan

Much of the agricultural base for Puerto Rican food is not native to the island. Cattle, sugar, coffee, bananas, coconuts, plantains, citrus fruit, onions, garlic, potatoes, and tomatoes were all introduced to the island from other places. Island recipes reflect the highly integrated mix of cultures. Although many Spanish flavors and recipes are found in Puerto Rican cooking, the major influence in the food is native Caribbean.

Puerto Rican food is not too spicy. The base of a majority of native dishes is *sofrito,* a seasoning sauce made from pureed tomatoes, onions, garlic, green peppers, sweet red chili peppers, coriander, annatto seeds, and a handful of other spices. It might be compared with the mildest picante sauce used in the Southwest or the U.S. version of Italian tomato sauce. In Puerto Rico, meats are grilled, many foods are fried, and rice and beans are standard side dishes.

Pigeon Peas and Rice

Ingredients:

  4 tablespoons annatto oil (or olive oil)

  1 tablespoon brown sugar

  1 pound beef stew meat, cut up into cubes

  water

  1 cup white rice

  1/2 cup fresh pigeon peas
  (or black-eyed peas)

  1/2 cup coconut milk

  salt and pepper

Directions:

Heat the oil in a stew pot. With help from an adult, add the brown sugar and stir until it has almost caramelized. Be very careful not to burn the sugar. Add the beef and enough water to just cover the beef. Bring to a boil, lower the heat, and then simmer until the meat is half cooked or for about 15 minutes.

Add the rice, peas, and coconut milk, and simmer for 20 minutes. Remove the pot from the heat, cover it, and let it sit for 15 minutes. Add salt and pepper to taste, and then serve.

Culture, Heritage, and History

Food is a central part of Puerto Rican's holiday and festival celebrations. These celebrations reflect the rich and varied cultural background and history of the island. Every city, town, and village in Puerto Rico celebrates its patron saint's day. Called *fiestas patronales*, a saint's day festival is the biggest event of the year in many towns and may last from three days to two weeks.

Official holidays celebrate events in both United States and Puerto Rican history. The island celebrates Presidents' Day and

Martin Luther King Day. It also celebrates the birth of Luis Muñoz Rivera and José de Diego. Columbus Day is celebrated, but so is Discovery Day. Columbus Day (October 12) commemorates the voyage of 1492; Discovery Day (November 19) marks the day Columbus discovered Puerto Rico in 1493. Christmas is celebrated on December 25, but Three Kings' Day is also celebrated on January 6. Three Kings' Day is a Spanish tradition that celebrates the coming of the Magi and marks the end of the winter holiday season.

Three Kings' Day is celebrated after Christmas.

CHAPTER TEN

Activity and Creativity

Sports have been a part of life in Puerto Rico since the native peoples built their first ceremonial ball courts and played a game similar to soccer. Soccer is still played here, and Puerto Rico has its own Olympic soccer team.

The favorite sport of Puerto Ricans, however, is baseball. Some of the best players in baseball history were born in Puerto Rico. The island's professional baseball teams play in the Caribbean League, where they face teams from Venezuela, Mexico, and the Dominican Republic. The league's season runs from October to March, with games played almost every day.

Fans in the United States have enjoyed the playing skill of a number of Puerto Rican baseball players. Orlando Cepeda, born in Ponce, played for the former New York Giants. In 1999, he became the second Puerto Rican inducted into the Baseball Hall of Fame. The first was Roberto Clemente.

Baseball is a Puerto Rican passion.

Basketball is also popular in Puerto Rico. The large cities have teams that play in Puerto Rico's national basketball federation, the Federación Nacional de Baloncesto de Puerto Rico.

Other popular spectator sports are tennis, boxing, cockfighting, and horse racing. Cockfighting has been popular in Puerto Rico for centuries, and the cockpits draw crowds of men in every city and

Opposite: Inside the Ponce Museum of Art

Roberto Clemente

Roberto Clemente Walker (listed as Roberto Walker Clemente in U.S. baseball records) is remembered as one of the best all-around baseball players in history. Born in Carolina in 1934, he was playing for the Santurce team when the Brooklyn Dodgers discovered him in 1954. The Pittsburgh Pirates soon claimed him, and he led that team to two World Series wins. Recognized as the National League's Most Valuable Player in 1966, Clemente won four National League batting championships and achieved a career record of 3,000 major-league hits. He died in a plane crash in 1972, while on a mission to help earthquake victims in Nicaragua. He was elected to the Baseball Hall of Fame the following year. The Roberto Clemente Sports City is dedicated to helping deprived children. ■

Puerto Rico has some of the best golf courses in the world.

town. As the roosters fight to the death, people bet on which bird will survive. Sometimes the betting is more frenzied than the fight.

Golf is a popular individual sport. The courses around the island rank with the best in the world. Both the ladies' and men's Senior PGA Tours finish their seasons in Puerto Rico. Famed professional golfer Juan Chi Chi Rodriguez is a native of Río Pedras.

Another world-class individual sports opportunity around the island is surfing. Puerto Rico hosted the world championships in 1968. Surfers find, however, that they must share the waves with boating enthusiasts. Fajardo is a sailing and yachting mecca. Yachting crews with serious intentions in the America's Cup races often practice near this popular port.

There is both freshwater and saltwater fishing around Puerto Rico. Twelve man-made lakes offer excellent sport fishing, especially for bass anglers. Those people looking for the "big one" prefer saltwater fishing. That usually means marlin, mackerel, sailfish, barracuda, and swordfish. Thirty world fishing records have been set in the waters surrounding the island.

Festival of Architectural Styles

Puerto Rico has a festival of architecture. From Spanish grillwork to modern steel-and-glass structures, Puerto Rican architecture reflects the island's diverse heritage and appreciation of both the beautiful and the absurd. The Columbus Quincentennial (500th anniversary of Columbus's arrival in the Americas) brought about a refurbishing of the island's colonial architecture. The major focus of this effort was centered in Old San Juan and Ponce.

Old San Juan's historic buildings have been protected from the elements of the open sea by the city walls, so many sixteenth-century structures have survived. Built in the sixteenth century, La Fortaleza was originally a medieval-style fortress and later became the governor's mansion. Like El Morro, La Fortaleza is a world heritage site, which puts the two forts in a class with the pyramids of Egypt and the Taj Mahal in India.

Twentieth-century restorations in Ponce included the neo-classic Casa Armstrong, Castillo Serralles, and Casa Villaronga. Casa Villaronga was home to Ponce architect Alfredo Wiecherms. It is a good example of the elegance and fun of the city's unique architecture. The most absurd architectural restoration in Ponce is a Victorian firehouse, the Parque de Bombas, the city's most photographed building. Painted in vivid red, green, black, and

La Fortaleza is a world heritage site.

*San Juan
Nepomuceno,
an oil painting
by José Campeche*

yellow stripes, it is Victorian gingerbread architecture out of control.

Arts and Artists

It is said that art depicts the soul of a nation. Puerto Rico's premier artists, José Campeche and Francisco Oller y Cestero, seemed to accomplish this.

The self-taught artist José Campeche, the son of a freed slave and an immigrant from the Canary Islands, was born in San Juan in 1752. He never left the island, but was greatly influenced by a Spanish court painter banished to Puerto Rico. He made his own paints from the juices of plants and flowers. The bulk of his work was painted on wood or copper rather than canvas. Many of his works were done for churches, though only about fifty remain. He created the main altar of the Church of Santa Ana in San Juan. He was also a popular portrait painter of Puerto Rican aristocrats and politicians.

Francisco Oller y Cestero, born in Bayamón in 1833, was

Ponce Museum of Art

Opened in 1966, the Ponce Museum of Art has a collection of more than 1,800 works of art by European masters, as well as paintings by the celebrated masters of Puerto Rico. A dream of industrialist Luis Ferré, it was founded in 1959 and moved into its present building in 1966. Designed by American architect Edward Durrell Stone, the museum displays the finest collection of art in the Caribbean. The building is a honeycomb of sunlit galleries entered by a scallop-shaped wooden central staircase. Some of the Old Masters represented in these galleries include Van Dyck, Rubens, Velazquez, and Gainsborough. Puerto Rican painters José Campeche and Francisco Oller are also featured The museum also has more than 400 sculptures in galleries throughout the building and in three garden areas.

trained by Europeans in Spain and France. His regional scenes show customs and folklore, reflecting the soul of his island home. One of his best-known works—*El velorio*, or *The Wake*—is filled with people mourning the loss of a child.

Other Puerto Rican artists are Lorenzo Homar and Ramón Frade. Frade's painting *El Jíbaro* is a tribute to the island's peasant farmers.

Literature and Life

Puerto Rican literature tells the story of the island's people, though this did not truly begin until the nineteenth century. The Spaniards had long repressed literature, fearing that writers would stir up revolution. But they could not keep Puerto Rican literature down. Writers such as Manuel A. Alonso, Eugenio María de Hostos, and Manuel Zeno Gandia wrote about the beauty and the hardships of life on the island.

Literary romanticism continued into the twentieth century. Virgilio Dávila's book *Pueblito de antes* (*Little Town of Long Ago*) was published in 1917. It is a nostalgic, romanticized look at the ordinary life of a small Puerto Rican village.

Luis Lloréns Torres, a much-admired poet, celebrated the heritage of the Caribbean. A collection of the poet's work, *Alturas de América* (*Heights of America*) was published in 1940.

By the 1930s, the literary vision of life on the island had turned dark. A group of writers known as Generación del 30 wrote about the Puerto Rican experience, the misery of the rural areas, and social justice. Writers Antonio Pedreira, Emilio Belaval, Tomás Blanco, and Enrique Laguerre were among the writers in this group. Members of Generación del 30 wrote around the theme of nationalism versus colonialism. José L. Gonzalez, René Marqués, and Pedro J. Soto wrote about emigration, war, and the Puerto Rican economy.

René Marqués, Puerto Rico's leading playwright, is known for plays that illuminate Puerto Rican life. One play, *Palm Sunday,* deals with the Ponce Massacre.

Late in the twentieth century, writers began to explore not only life on the island, but also life for Puerto Ricans in the United States. Piri Thomas's autobiography, *Down These Mean Streets,* published in 1967, depicts the experience of dislocation many Puerto Ricans feel as they try to adjust to life on the mainland.

Soul Music

The music of Puerto Rico reflects the blend of many cultures. Harmonies of Spanish religious music backed by rhythms with a strong African beat and accompanied by instruments first used by the island's native peoples add up to a music that speaks to the Puerto Rican soul.

The instruments that play this "soul" music are also a unique mix. The Taíno people created percussion instruments from gourds, which included gourd rattles, called maracas, and long, hollow gourds played with a stick, called güiros. Deprived of their traditional stringed instruments, early Spanish settlers created their own. Africans added their drums and rhythms. Throw in a few trumpets and anything else that makes a sound, and Puerto Ricans can make music.

Plena is part of most Puerto Rican festivals.

The tradition of makeshift instruments is the basis for a music style called *plena*. A plena is a wild, rhythmic dance accompanied by a group of young men playing a variety of hand-held, often homemade, instruments called *pleneras* or *panderetas*. Plena originated with Africans in Ponce. Now it is a staple of the island's patron saint festivals and hotel entertainments. Like American jazz, plena is a free style of music that also has a written form. César Concepción and Rafael Cortijo are known for their plena compositions. Cortijo made many records in the 1950s and 1960s that sold well around the world.

Another uniquely Puerto Rican music, is *danza*, a music that was first enjoyed by the Puerto Rican aristocracy in the nineteenth century. Today, woodwind and string orchestras play the music in a concert setting—for everyone.

The real soul music of Puerto Rico, however, is salsa. It is a spicy blend of African and Caribbean music played American big-band jazz style. A salsa group is composed of a lead singer, backed by a small chorus, and a band of piano, bass, horn section, and a heavy assortment of percussion instruments that include the bongos, conga, maracas, and a cowbell. Puerto Rican bandleader Tito Puente, one of the originators of salsa, introduced this spicy music to the mainland. Willie Colón, Ray Barreto, and José Feliciano helped popularize this music in the 1970s.

Puerto Ricans also enjoy classical European forms of music. The island has an active opera company and probably the best sym-

Puerto Rico native Tito Puente is a jazz drummer and bandleader.

phony orchestra in the Caribbean. Cellist Pablo Casals is the person responsible for the revival of interest in European classical music in modern Puerto Rico.

Theater and Dance

There is a theatrical tradition in Puerto Rico backed by the island's government. Classic works of drama, including plays from the Spanish theater repertory and modern American drama, are presented in Spanish. Most of the larger cities have theaters.

Founded in 1987, a company called Productora de Teatro Nacional travels islandwide offering hundreds of performances a year. Six theater groups and two dance troupes are associated with this corporation.

The San Juan Ballet performs with the Symphony Orchestra at the Centro de Bellas Artes in Santurce. The San Juan City Ballet performs at the restored Tapia y Rivera Theater in Old San Juan. Modern dance is performed at the Julia de Burgos Amphitheater

Pablo Casals

Born in Vendrell, Spain, in 1876, to a Puerto Rican mother, Pablo Casals was one of the greatest musicians of the twentieth century. His instrument was the cello, but he was also a conductor, composer, and teacher. He modernized cello technique and established the cello as a solo instrument.

While visiting his mother in Puerto Rico in 1956, he decided to stay, because life in Spain under General Francisco Franco was not good. Governor Luis Muñoz Marín invited the cellist to establish a festival in Puerto Rico. The first Casals Music Festival was held in San Juan in 1957. Casals founded and conducted the Puerto Rico Symphony Orchestra. He also established the Puerto Rican Conservatory of Music. He died in 1973. ■

Actress Rita Moreno gained fame on stage and screen.

in Río Piedras as part of the University of Puerto Rico cultural activities.

Puerto Rican actors and entertainers have found fame on Broadway and in Hollywood. Actor José Ferrer, probably best known for his 1952 role as artist Henri de Toulouse-Lautrec in the film *Moulin Rouge,* was born in Santurce. Rita Moreno, born in Humacao, became a star after she appeared in the movie version of the Broadway musical *West Side Story*. Still active in movies and television, she was the first performer to win all the major awards: an Oscar, an Emmy, a Grammy, and a Tony award. Born in San Juan, Raúl Julia became a noted actor on Broadway as well as in Hollywood. Not long before he died of a heart attack at the height of his career in 1994, he had become popular as the father in *The Addams Family* movies.

As the twenty-first century started, the most popular Puerto Rican entertainer was Ricky (Enrique) Martin. Born in San Juan, he got his start in the 1980s with the singing group Menudo before going solo. Martin's act fills large theaters and arenas all over the world.

In the arts, entertainment, and sports, there is no question of status. In this area of Puerto Rican life, it is a matter of talent and dedication.

Ricky Martin accepting a Grammy Award

Timeline

United States History

Puerto Rico's History

1493 Christopher Columbus lands in Borinquén and renames it San Juan Bautista.

1508 Ponce de León sails to the island and founds Caparra.

1513 Spain authorizes the use of African slaves in the colony.

1532–40 La Fortaleza fortress is built.

1539 Construction on El Morro is begun.

1585 Led by Sir Francis Drake, English troops invade San Juan Bautista.

1598 Englishman George Clifford lays siege to San Juan Bautista, then burns it down.

The first permanent English settlement is established in North America at Jamestown. **1607**

Pilgrims found Plymouth Colony, the second permanent English settlement. **1620**

1625 Dutch sailors invade the city then destroy it.

America declares its independence from Britain. **1776**

The Treaty of Paris officially ends the Revolutionary War in America. **1783**

The U.S. Constitution is written. **1787**

The Louisiana Purchase almost doubles the size of the United States. **1803**

The United States and Britain fight the War of 1812. **1812–15**

1783 The wall surrounding San Juan Bautista is completed in an effort to keep out invaders.

1812 The Constitution of 1812 is drafted, giving Puerto Ricans basic civil rights.

1814 King Ferdinand of Spain removes the constitution and strips Puerto Ricans of their rights.

1849 Spanish-appointed governor, Juan de Pezuelas, places restrictions on agricultural workers and ends most forms of entertainment for Puerto Ricans.

United States History

The North and South fight **1861–65** each other in the American Civil War.

The United States is **1917–18** involved in World War I.

The stock market crashes, **1929** plunging the United States into the Great Depression.

The United States **1941–45** fights in World War II.

The United States becomes a **1945** charter member of the U.N.

The United States **1951–53** fights in the Korean War.

The U.S. Congress enacts a series of **1964** groundbreaking civil rights laws.

The United States **1964–73** engages in the Vietnam War.

The United States and other **1991** nations fight the brief Persian Gulf War against Iraq.

Puerto Rico's History

1855 Cholera kills 30,000 Puerto Ricans.

1868 Puerto Rican revolutionaries capture Lares and form the Republic of Puerto Rico.

1873 Slavery is abolished in Puerto Rico.

1898 The Autonomic Charter of 1897 goes into effect. The United States invades the island on July 25. Under the Treaty of Paris, Puerto Rico falls under U.S. rule.

1900 Puerto Rico's basic government is formed under the Foraker Act.

1917 The Jones Act is passed granting Puerto Ricans U.S. citizenship.

1928 A hurricane destroys coffee and sugar plantations on the island.

1938 The Popular Democratic Party is formed by Luis Muñoz Marín.

1947 The Butler-Crawford Bill is passed, amending the Jones Act.

1952 Puerto Rico's commonwealth status goes into effect under Public Law 600 on July 25.

1967 Puerto Rican voters cast nonbinding status vote.

1998 Voters cast another vote on Puerto Rico's status.

Fast Facts

The capitol

Coquí

Official name	Commonwealth of Puerto Rico, or Estado Libre Asociado de Puerto Rico
Commonwealth date	July 25, 1952
Puerto Rico's capital	San Juan
Motto	John Is His Name, or *Joannes Est Nomen Eius*, referring to St. John the Baptist
Puerto Rico's bird	Stripe-headed tanager, or *reinita mora*
Puerto Rico's flower	Puerto Rican hibiscus, or *flor de maga*
Puerto Rico's song	"La Borinqueña"
Puerto Rico's tree	Silk-cotton tree, or ceiba
Puerto Rico's animal	Coquí, a tree frog

San Juan

Total area	3,515 sq. mi. (9,104 sq km), including Culebra, Mona, and Vieques Islands
Land area	3,459 sq. mi. (8,959 sq km)
Inland water area	56 sq. mi. (145 sq km)
Coastline	311 miles (500 km)
Tidal shoreline	700 miles (1,126 km), including bays and inlets
Latitude and longitude	Puerto Rico, including Culebra, Mona, and Viesques Islands, is located approximately between 18° 00′ and 18° 30′ N, and 65° 15′ and 67° 15′ W
Highest point	Cerro de Punta, 4,389 feet (1,339 m)
Lowest point	Sea level along the Atlantic Ocean
Largest city	San Juan
Number of districts	8
Population	3,808,610 (2000 census)
Density	1,101 persons per sq. mi. (425 per sq km)
Population distribution	67% urban, 33% rural

Ethnic distribution (does not equal 100%)		
White		80.5%
African-American		8.0%
Other		6.8%

Record high temperature	103°F (39°C) at San Lorenzo on August 22, 1906
Record low temperature	40°F (4°C) at Aibonito on March 9, 1911

Puerto Rican girls

Average July temperature	80°F (27°C)
Average January temperature	73°F (23°C)
Average annual precipitation	70 inches (178 cm) in the north; 37 inches (94 cm) in the south

El Morro

Natural Areas and Historic Sites

Historic Sites

San Juan National Historic Site offers tours of the three fortresses built during the sixteenth century to protect the island from invaders.

The Capitol is the home of the country's legislature. It displays Puerto Rico's constitution along with many other historical memorabilia.

Casa Blanca, or the White House, the home of explorer Juan Ponce de León, became the residence of various Spanish commanders, and then the home of the U.S. commander of Puerto Rico.

Casa de las Contrafuertes, or House of Buttresses, contains a drugstore from the nineteenth century as well as exhibits of Latin American prints.

San Juan Cathedral holds the tomb of Juan Ponce de León within its impressive architecture.

Wilderness Parks

Cabezas de San Juan Nature Preserve in northeastern Puerto Rico includes beaches, swamps, and a forest. Visitors to the preserve can see many endangered species here and tour El Faro.

Caribbean National Forest

Cabo Rojo National Wildlife Refuge in the southwestern portion of Puerto Rico has a visitors' center and many outstanding opportunities for bird-watching.

Guánica Forest Reserve is of special interest to tree enthusiasts, who can see forty-eight rare species of trees in this dry forest, as well as many types of birds.

Parks

Muñoz Marín Park in Hato Rey, San Juan, allows visitors to picnic along its beautiful lakes. These are also presentations on the park's animals and plants.

Luis A. Ferré Park in San Juan offers many educational opportunities for sightseers, including museums, rocket displays, and a zoo.

Forests

Caribbean National Forest, also known as El Yunque, is the only tropical forest in the National Forest System and the home of rare wildlife, such as the Puerto Rican parrot.

Cloud Forest has a high altitude of 2,500 to 3,500 feet (763 to 1,068 m) and is continually wet from precipitation. It has interesting flora, such as dwarfed, vine-covered trees, and a wealth of animal life.

Piñones Forest has the largest mangrove area in the country.

Smaller Islands

Culebra is a Caribbean paradise, with its white sandy beaches. Snorkelers and divers can enjoy the island's clear water, and nature lovers can see giant sea turtles, waterbirds, and mangrove forests.

Vieques is also a vacationer's dream. The marine plankton is a remarkable sight. It glows when it is disturbed and looks magical at night. Other sights include a fort—Spain's last construction in the Americas—and a lighthouse.

Cultural Institutions

Libraries

Biblioteca Madre María Teresa Guevara, or the Mother Maria Teresa Guevara Library, is at Sagrado Corazón University. It has many special collections, including the Puerto Rican Collection, Historical Archives, and the Foundation Center Collection.

The General Library at the University of Puerto Rico's Mayagüez Campus has several collections, including the Puerto Rico Collection, Government Documents Collection, and the Marine Sciences Special Collection.

Museums

El Museo de Arte Contemporáneo de Puerto Rico, or the Museum of Contemporary Puerto Rican Art, has a permanent collection of art by Puerto Rican, Caribbean, and Central and South American artists.

El Museo de las Américas, or the Museum of the Americas, in San Juan used to be the home of Spanish troops. It now has permanent exhibits on popular art movements from North, Central, and South America, as well as the Caribbean.

The Museum of Puerto Rican Music in Ponce has memorabilia of the region's music, along with exhibits on Indian, Spanish, and African instruments.

The Taíno Museum has more than 200 pieces of art by the Taíno Indians, who were the majority in the eastern Caribbean prior to Columbus's arrival.

Performing Arts

Puerto Rico has many professional arts companies, including those of the *Ballet Concierto de Puerto Rico* (The Puerto Rican Concert Ballet).

Universities and Colleges

Puerto Rico has sixty-nine public and private institutions of higher learning.

University of Puerto Rico

Annual Events

January–March

Three Kings' Day (January 6)

Eugenio María de Hostos birthday (January 11)

Carnaval in Ponce (February)

Coffee Harvest Festival in Maricao (February)

Dulce Sueno Paso Fino Horse Show in Guayama (late February to early March)

Heineken Regatta, first part of the Caribbean Ocean Racing Triangle (March)

Emancipation Day (March 22)

April–June

José de Diego birthday celebration (April 16)

Heineken Jazz Festival in San Juan (May)

Casals Carnaval in San Juan (mid-June)

Bomba y Plena Festival in Ponce (June)

Aibonito Flower Festival (June)

Eve of San Juan Bautista Day (June 23)

July–September

Barranquitas Artisans Fair (mid-July)

Loíza Festival (late July)

Inter-American Festival of the Arts in San Juan (September–October)

October–December

Columbus Day (October 12)

Puerto Rican Music Festival in San Juan (November–December)

Jayuya Indian Festival (November)

Discovery Day (November 19)

Hatillo Festival of the Masks (late December)

**Roberto Walker
Clemente**

Ricky Martin

Famous People

Pedro Albizu Campos (1893–1965)	Politician
Manuel A. Alonso y Pacheco (1822–1899)	Author and physician
Félix Astol y Artés (1813–1901)	Musician
José Campeche (1752–1809)	Artist
Pablo Casals (1876–1973)	Cellist and composer
José Celso Barbosa (1857–1921)	Politician and physician
Roberto Walker Clemente (1934–1972)	Baseball player
Christopher Columbus (1451–1506)	Explorer
José Cruz Jr. (1974–)	Baseball player
María Dadilla de Martínez (1884?–1951)	Essayist and folklorist
José de Diego (1866–1918)	Politician and poet
José Feliciano (1945–)	Singer
Luis A. Ferré (1904–)	Politician
José Ferrer (1912–1992)	Actor
Juan Ramón Jiménez (1881–1958)	Poet
Raúl Julia (1940–1994)	Actor
Ricky Martin (1971–)	Singer and actor
Rosendo Matienzo Cintrón (1855–1913)	Attorney and social reformer
Rita Moreno (1931–)	Actress, dancer, and singer
Luis Muñoz Marín (1898–1980)	Politician
Luis Muñoz Rivera (1859–1916)	Newspaper editor and politician
Antonia C. Novello (1944–)	Physician and former surgeon general

Rosie Perez (1964–)	Actor
Jesús T. Piñero (1897–1952)	Politician
Tito Puente (1923–)	Jazz musician
Chita Rivera (1933–)	Actor and singer
Geraldo Rivera (1943–)	Journalist
Segundo Ruiz Belvis (1829–1867)	Statesman
Jimmy Smits (1955–)	Actor

Tito Puente

To Find Out More

History

- Aliotta, Jerome. *The Puerto Rican Americans*. Broomall, Penn.: Chelsea House, 1995.

- Fradin, Dennis Brindell. *Puerto Rico*. Danbury, Conn.: Children's Press, 1995.

- Harlan, Judith. *Puerto Rico: Deciding Its Future*. New York: Twenty-First Century Books, 1996.

- Johnston, Joyce. *Puerto Rico*. Minneapolis: Lerner Publications, 1994.

- Thompson, Kathleen. *Puerto Rico*. Austin, Tex.: Raintree/Steck Vaughn, 1996.

Biography

- Bernier-Grand, Carmen T. *Poet and Politician of Puerto Rico: Don Luis Muñoz Marín*. New York: Orchard Books, 1995.

- George, Linda and Charles. *Luis Muñoz Marín*. Danbury, Conn.: Children's Press, 1999.

- Suntree, Susan. *Rita Moreno*. Broomall, Penn.: Chelsea House, 1992.

- Walker, Paul Robert. *Pride of Puerto Rico: The Life of Roberto Clemente*. San Diego: Harcourt Brace, 1988.

Fiction

- Bernier-Grand, Carmen T. *In the Shade of the Nispero Tree*. New York: Orchard Books, 1999.

- Mike, Jan M., and Charles Reasoner (illustrator). *Juan Bobo and the Horse of Seven Colors: A Puerto Rican Legend*. Mahwah, N.J.: Troll, 1995.

Websites

■ **Office of the Governor**
http://fortaleza.govpr.org/
For information on the
country's highest official

■ **Senate of Puerto Rico**
http://www.senado
pr.us.org
For information on all
aspects of the common-
wealth's senate

■ **The University of Puerto
Rico**
http://www.upr.clu.edu/upri
For information on the
commonwealth's largest
university

Addresses

■ **The Museum of the
Americas**
Edificio Cuartel Ballajá
Apartado S-4467
San Juan, PR 00902-4467
For information about this
popular museum

■ **Puerto Rican Tourism
Company**
La Princesa Building #2
Paseo La Princesa
Old San Juan, PR 00902
For information on activities
in Puerto Rico

Index

Page numbers in *italics* indicate illustrations.

Meet the Author

Lucile Davis has written many nonfiction books for children. She is the author of *Alabama*, also in the America the Beautiful series. She holds a bachelor's degree in English from the University of Missouri at St. Louis and a master's degree in theater from Texas Christian University.

Lucile Davis did most of her research for this book at the library, on the telephone, and on the Internet. The Honorable Carlos Romero Barceló and his staff in Washington, D.C., were particularly helpful. Also, she had special help from the office staff of the Honorable Kay Granger in Fort Worth, Texas, in researching the issue of Puerto Rico's status referendum.

Websites run by the office of the governor, the senate of Puerto Rico, and the University of Puerto Rico provided valuable information about the commonwealth. Another useful website for bibliographic references and links is the "Welcome to Puerto Rico" site maintained by Magaly Rivera, a native of Puerto Rico.

However, Davis says the best way to get to know Puerto Rico is to go there. Lucile Davis is a native Texan and lives in Fort Worth.

Photo Credits

Photographs ©:

AKG London: 123
Archive Photos: 12, 13, 52 (Ana Martínez/Reuters), 53 (Toshio Sakai/Reuters), 23, 27, 39, 41, 44, 124
Art Resource, NY: 118 (National Museum of American Art, Smithsonian Institution, Washington, DC/Collection of Teodoro Vidal)
Bridgeman Art Library International Ltd., London/New York: 14 (IND113076/The Landing of Christopher Columbus on the island of San Salvador on the 12th October 1492, from The Discovery of America; pub. Barcelona, 1878 by Spanish School, 19th century/ Private Collection/Index.), 15 (HTD75433/ Map of the island of Puerto Rico, 1599 by Samuel de Champlain, Royal Common-wealth Society, London, UK.), 19 (IND113069/The "Pinta", the "Niña" and the "Santa María" sailing towards the East Indies in 1492, from The Discovery of America, pub. Barcelona, 1878 by Spanish School, 19th century/Private Collection/Index.), 22 (JAL61778/Ferdinand VII by Luis López Piquer, Academia de San Fernando, Madrid)
Corbis-Bettmann: 84, 128 top (John Dakers/Eye Ubiquitous), 122, 135 (Craig Lovell), 125, 134 bottom (Pacha), 92 top (The Purcell Team), 38, 47, 49, 51, 86 top (UPI), 48, 116 top, 134 top
D. Donne Bryant Stock Photography: 95 (Robert Fried), 17, 85, 121, 133 (Suzanne L. Murphy-Larronde)
Envision: 112 (Peter Johansky)
James Marshall: 6 top left, 76

Kevin Schafer: 6 bottom, 92 bottom, 128 bottom
Latin Focus: back cover, 60, 69, 71, 74, 81, 86 bottom, 94, 98, 99, 114 (Mark Bacon)
Len Kaufman: 56, 66, 117
Liaison Agency, Inc.: 29, 31 (Hulton Getty), 108 (Mark Lewis), 91 (Michael Massey), 54, 110, 131 (Larry Mayer)
Mark Bacon: 62, 65 bottom, 72, 83, 92 top right, 97, 113, 116 bottom
New England Stock Photo: 2 (Thomas R. Fletcher)
North Wind Picture Archives: 32, 36, 37
Peter Arnold Inc.: 87, 104
Photo Researchers: 65 top (James W. Wiley/National Audubon Society)
Robert Fried Photography: 70, 78, 103, 129 top
Stock Montage, Inc.: 24, 34
Superstock, Inc.: 18, 42
Suzanne Murphy-Larronde: 7 top right, 107, 129 bottom
The Image Works: 77 (Tony Arruza), 111 (Townsend P. Dickinson), 101, 119 (Macduff Everton)
Tony Stone Images: 6 top right, 61 (Tom Bean), 68, 130 (Michelle & Tom Grimm), 8 (Bill Hinsohn), cover (Mark Lewis), 7 top left, 67 (Stuart Westmorland)
Viesti Collection, Inc.: 9 (Martha Cooper)
Visuals Unlimited: 63 (Jeffrey Howe)
Wolfgang Kaehler: 6 top center, 55, 105
Woodfin Camp & Associates: 80 (Bernard Boutrit), 7 top center, 58, 82, 102, 109, 132 (Robert Frerck), 7 bottom, 115 (Stephanie Maze)
Maps by XNR Productions, Inc.